The
Graying
of the
Church

**A Leader's Guide for Older-Adult Ministry
in The United Methodist Church**

Richard H. Gentzler, Jr., D.Min.

Director, Center on Aging and Older-Adult Ministries
General Board of Discipleship
The United Methodist Church

DISCIPLESHIP RESOURCES

PO BOX 340003 • NASHVILLE, TN 37203-0003
www.discipleshipresources.org

The Graying of the Church is dedicated to the thousands of men and women, both clergy and lay, in The United Methodist Church who provide a ministry of programs and support for the Christian faith formation and spiritual well-being of older adults.

Cover and book design by Nanci H. Lamar
Edited by Linda R. Whited and Heidi L. Hewitt

ISBN 0-88177-409-X
Library of Congress Control Number 2003106216

DR409

Contents

Introduction

In 1900, life expectancy in the United States was 47. Today, the figure is closer to 77, and we are likely to remain active and in good health for most of that time. Although more people are living longer lives, the real revolution is yet to be felt. By 2010, people 60 or older will outnumber children and youth under 15. Beginning in 2010—when the first wave of the Baby Boomer Generation (born 1946–1964) begins reaching age 65—and continuing to 2030, the U.S. population 65 years or older is expected to grow by about 43.5% to about 70 million, making up more than 20% of the total population. About one in five people will be 65 years or older. As a result of this growing older population, people 65 years or older are expected to outnumber children and youth under age 18 by 2030.

But what are the implications on public life for such an expanding aging society? Simply put, the implications are dramatic and profound. With vast numbers of elderly, there will be a major increase in the numbers of people requiring special services (health, housing, and so forth). Greater numbers will be participating in various entitlement programs, and many more will be requiring formal and informal care. Such an impact will be felt for the whole range of our social institutions, from education and family to business, government, and religion.

It is not news that The United Methodist Church membership is aging, too. Approximately 62% of our membership is 50 years or older, and the average age of our membership is nearly 60. This is not necessarily a bad sign, or a sign of impending doom. It is, however, a warning that the church must reconsider its priority for ministry.

Just as American businesses are realizing that the growing numbers of older adults demand a retooling of their marketing strategy, The United Methodist Church must realize that the graying of the church demands a retooling of its ministry strategy. Much has been made of this reality in the past several years, and many churches have begun developing intentional ministries aimed at serving the older segment of their membership.

But while we have begun to explore the needs, interests, and requirements of our older members, few churches fully understand the extent to which the makeup of the population in the future will differ from that which we have traditionally understood. Even more important is that we are not really aware of the profound impact the population shift will have on our ministry. With so many congregations experiencing a population boom of elderly, and many having fewer and fewer children and young people, we need to rethink and refocus our priority for ministry. While the church must be engaged in outreach and evangelism with people of all ages (children, youth, young adults, families, singles, couples, and people at midlife), it must also recognize that a viable ministry for the future is an intentional ministry by, with, and for older adults.

Yet, this is not as simple as it may at first seem. Many leaders believe that unless churches are overflowing with young people, they are dead or dying. Like it or not, almost all of us have absorbed the extremely negative model of aging that arose as a result of the Industrial Revolution and its insidious message that we are all worth only as much as we produce. Older adults are often stereotyped as poor, isolated, sick, unhappy, and desolate or are viewed as controlling, rigid, and unchanging. These negative stereotypes of old age are part of our culture's obsession with youth and our fear of aging and death. Our society's negative attitude toward and image of older adults can be referred to as ageism, which means stereotyping and discriminating against people because they are older.

Obviously, it is true that churches may be dying if they are not about their primary task of making new disciples of Jesus Christ and bringing in new young members. Churches must be engaged in the primary task of reaching out and inviting all people into its fellowship, relating them to God through Jesus Christ, nurturing them in the Christian faith, and equipping and supporting them to live as Christian disciples. This primary task is the mission of The United Methodist Church, but it is also the mission of older-adult ministries. The mission of older-adult ministries must be in alignment with the mission of the church and include reaching, relating, nurturing, and equipping older adults.

A church filled with older adults does not necessarily mean that it is dead or dying. Nor does it mean that ministry cannot happen in that setting. Older adults present society and our churches with a variety of challenges, but they also bring tremendous resources that cannot be ignored. In many situations, older adults will be the growing (and primary) population in our communities. It may well be that with the growing numbers of older adults, God has a particular purpose or plan in mind for the church. If God has provided us with increasing longevity, we can ill afford to ignore so great a population. Neither can we afford to allow the faith, wisdom, and experience that often abounds in older adults to be lost or underutilized.

This book is intended to help church leaders gain a better perspective on ministry with older adults. Its primary purpose is to provide the tools and knowledge for equipping church leaders who want to be engaged in older-adult ministries. The church has the opportunity to reframe the experience of aging and help cultivate among older adults the qualities of spiritual maturity: love, joy, peace, patience, kindness, generosity, faithfulness, gentleness, and self-control (Galatians 5:22-23). My sincere hope is that this book will create a clear understanding of our graying population and will provide a valuable resource for leaders who want to be intentional in their ministry by, with, and for older adults.

CHAPTER 1

Demographics
of Our Older
Population

More people are living longer than ever before. Medical advances have greatly reduced infant mortality and death from childhood diseases. As a result, people have a greater chance of surviving the first years of life. In addition, new medical knowledge, life-sustaining technologies, and a greater awareness of, and desire for, a healthy lifestyle have also helped lengthen the lives of those who do reach old age.

In this chapter, we will look at the makeup of older adults in our society. The statistical data is drawn from *A Profile of Older Americans: 2001,* which was produced by the Administration on Aging. As we gain an awareness of the aging population in the United States, we will have a better understanding of the impact this growing population will have on our church.

DEMOGRAPHICS

The older-adult population—people 65 years or older—numbers 35 million. They represent approximately 12.4% of the U.S. population, or about one of every eight Americans. The number of older Americans has increased by 12% (or 3.7 million) since 1990, compared with an increase of 13.3% for the under-65 population. By 2030, when all members of the Baby Boomer Generation (born 1946–1964) will have reached legal retirement age, more than 20% of Americans will be 65 years or older.

Today, there are approximately 20.6 million older women and 14.4 million older men, or a ratio of 143 women for every 100 men. The female-to-male ratio increases with age, starting at 117 women for every 100 men for the 65–69 group, to 245 women for every 100 men for those 85 years or older.

Since 1900, the percentage of Americans 65 years or older has more than tripled, from 4.1% in 1900 to 12.4% in 2000. The number of Americans 65 years or older has increased 11 times, from 3.1 million to 35 million.

The older population itself is getting older. The 65–74 age group (18.4 million) is 8 times larger than in 1900. The 75–84 age group (12.4 million) is 16 times larger, and the 85 years or older age group (4.2 million) is 34 times larger. People reaching age 65 have an average life expectancy of 17.9 additional years (19.2 years for females and 16.3 years for males). The proportion of Americans age 60 with at least one parent alive has risen from 7% in 1900 to 44% in 2000.

A child born at the turn of the twenty-first century can expect to live about 30 years longer than a child born at the turn of the twentieth century. A major part of this increase is because of the reduced death rates for children and young adults.

More than two million people celebrated their sixty-fifth birthday in the year 2000 (5,574 per day). In the same year, about 1.8 million people 65 years or older died (4,924 per day), resulting in a net increase of approximately 238,000 (650 per day).

It is important to know that the older population will continue to grow significantly in the future, with the older population burgeoning between the years 2010 and 2030, when the Baby Boomer Generation reaches 65 years or older.

By 2030, there will be about 70 million older people, more than twice the present number. People 65 years or older represent 12.4% of the U.S. population today but will grow to nearly 20% of the population by 2030. According to the U.S. Census Bureau's projections, by 2030 adults 65 years or older will outnumber children and youth under age 18 (22% versus 21%). Projections indicate that as early as 2010, adults 60 years or older will outnumber children and youth under 15 (19.4% versus 18.9%).

Not only is our population aging but more of our oldest adults are living longer, too. The number of centenarians (100 years or older) in 2000 was 68,000. The number is expected to increase to 131,000 in 2010, to 214,000 in 2020, to 324,000 in 2030, to 447,000 in 2040, and to 834,000 in 2050.

WHERE OLDER ADULTS LIVE

In 2000, 52% of the adults 65 years or older lived in nine states: California (3.6 million), Florida (2.8 million), New York (2.4 million), Texas (2.1 million), Pennsylvania (1.9 million), Ohio (1.5 million), Illinois (1.5 million), Michigan (1.2 million), and New Jersey (1.1 million). The four states with the fewest older adults each had fewer than 100,000: Alaska, North Dakota, Vermont, and Wyoming.

The majority (77.5%) of people 65 years or older lived in metropolitan areas in 2000. About 50% of older people lived in the suburbs, 27% lived in central cities, and 23% lived in non-metropolitan areas.

LIVING ARRANGEMENTS

The majority (67%) of older non-institutionalized adults live in a family setting. Approximately 10.8 million (80%) older men and 10.7 million (58%) older women live in families. The proportion living in a family setting decreases with age. Approximately 45% of those 85 years or older live in a family setting. About 13% of older adults (7% men, 17% women) are not living with a spouse but are living with children, siblings, or other relatives. An additional 3% of older men and 2% of older women (or 718,000 older adults) live with non-relatives.

About 30% (9.7 million—7.3 million women, 2.4 million men) of all non-institutionalized older adults lived alone in 2000. They represented 40% of older women and 17% of older men. Living alone correlates with advanced age. Among women who are 75 years or older, for example, about half (49.4%) lived alone.

While a small number (1.56 million) and percentage (4.5%) of the people 65 years or older live in nursing homes, the percentage increases dramatically with age, ranging from 1.1% for people 65–74 years to 4.7% for people 75–84 years and 18.2% for people 85 years or older.

MARITAL STATUS

More than half (55%) of older non-institutionalized adults lived with their spouse in 2000. Older men are much more likely to be married than older women: 73% of men, compared with 41% of women. Since women have a longer life expectancy than men (79.7 years at birth for women, compared with 74.3 years for men) and men often marry younger women, nearly half

(45%) of all older women are widows, with more than four times as many widows (8.5 million) as widowers (2 million). Only 28.8% of women 75 years or older lived with a spouse in 2000.

Divorced and separated older adults represent only 8% of the total older population. However, their numbers (2.6 million) have increased significantly since 1990, when approximately 1.5 million of the older population were divorced or separated.

RACE AND ETHNICITY

In 2000, 16.4% of people 65 years or older were minorities: African Americans, 8.0%; Asian Americans or Pacific Islanders, 2.4%; and Native Americans or Native Alaskans, less than 1%. People of Hispanic origin, who may be of any race (White, Black, Asian, and so forth), represented 5.6% of the older population. In addition, 0.8% of those 65 years or older identified themselves as being of two or more races. Minority populations are projected to represent 25.4% in 2030, up from 16.4% in 2000.

INCOME

The median income in 2000 for men 65 years or older was $19,168, while the median income for older women was almost half that amount ($10,899). Households containing families headed by people 65 years or older reported a median income of $32,854 ($33,467 for Whites, $27,952 for African Americans, and $24,330 for Hispanics). About 12.1% (or one of every eight) of family households with an elderly head had incomes less than $15,000, and 46.8% had incomes of $35,000 or more. Of the 21.4 million households headed by older adults, 80% were owners and 20% were renters.

The major sources of income for older adults are Social Security (90%), income from assets (62%), public and private pensions (43%), and earnings (22%). Social Security benefits account for 38% of the aggregate income of the older population. The bulk of the remainder consists of earnings (21%), assets (20%), and pensions (19%).

WORK FORCE

In 2000, 4.2 million Americans 65 years or older were in the labor force, including 2.4 million men (17.5%) and 1.8 million women (9.4%). About 12.8% of the total older-adult population (or one in eight) were either working or actively seeking work. Older adults made up 3% of the U.S. labor force. About 3.1% were unemployed. The number of working adults 65 years or older will increase to 10.1 million by 2030.

EDUCATION

Older adults have significantly less formal education than the younger generations have. Because education influences attitudes and values, this difference causes a gap between the oldest and youngest generations. Although a little more than 30% of people 65 years or older did not graduate from high school, the educational level of the older population is increasing. Between 1970 and 2000, the percentage who had completed high school rose from 28% to 70%. About 16% in 2000 had a bachelor's degree or more.

The percentage who had completed high school varied considerably by race and ethnic origin among older adults in 2000: 74% of Whites, 63% of Asian Americans and Pacific Islanders, 46% of African Americans, and 37% of Hispanics.

GRANDPARENTHOOD

While the onset age of grandparenthood may be significantly younger than age 65, it is worth noting that many older adults are grandparents. And, as such, the number of children living in the home of a grandparent has increased significantly, rising from 2.2 million in 1970 to 3.8 million in 2000. Roughly 5% of children were living with their grandparents in 2000, compared with 3% in 1970.

More than half (59%) of children living in a grandparent's home also have their mother or both parents living with them. But 1.4 million children (35%) live only with their grandparents.

Although grandparents are happy having grandchildren nearby, they often find it difficult having the children living with them. Grandparents who are raising grandchildren may need assistance and advice.

POVERTY RATES

The poverty rate for older adults continues to decrease. In 2000, 10.2% (3.4 million) of the older population lived below poverty level, compared with 24.6% in 1970. One of every twelve (8.9%) Whites are classified as poor, compared with one of every five (22.3%) African Americans and slightly fewer Hispanics

(18.8%). Higher than average poverty rates for older adults correlate with living in rural areas (13.2%), in the South (12.7%), and in central cities (12.4%).

Older women have a higher poverty rate (12.2%) than older men (7.5%). Older adults living alone or with non-relatives are much more likely to be poor (20.8%) than those who are living with families (5.1%). Older Hispanic women who live alone or with non-relatives experience the highest poverty rates (38.3%). Without Social Security, 48 percent of older adults would live in poverty.

The ten jurisdictions with the highest poverty rates for older adults are Mississippi (19.1%), Louisiana (17.1%), the District of Columbia (16.5%), Arkansas (15.8%), West Virginia (15.1%), New Mexico (14.8%), Texas (14.4%), Alabama (13.3%), New York (13.2%), and North Carolina (12.7%).

HEALTH

Nearly 74% of older adults 65 years or older assessed their health as excellent, very good, or good, while 26% indicated that their health was fair or poor. Among those 65–74 years old, 28.8% reported a limitation caused by a chronic condition. In contrast, more than half (50.6%) of those 75 years or older reported they were limited by chronic conditions. Most older adults have at least one chronic condition, and many have multiple conditions. The most frequently occurring conditions per 100 elderly in 1996 were arthritis (49), hypertension (36), hearing impairments (30), heart disease (27), cataracts (17), orthopedic impairments (18), sinusitis (12), and diabetes (10).

In summary, the myths of aging would have us conclude that all older adults are economically disadvantaged and physically frail. Many people believe that older adults are ready to disengage from society and are content to sit at home alone while waiting for death to release them from the confines of their misery. Yet, as we study the statistical data presented in this chapter, we see that the majority of adults 65 years or older are healthy, active, and involved in life. Our expectations suggest that we are often guilty of stereotyping older adults.

CHAPTER 2

Generational Differences of Midlife and Older Adults

The aging of America and the graying of The United Methodist Church will bring about a shift from a youth-oriented culture to a more mature one. As a result, our lives will change in ways we might now find hard to imagine. For example, the aging Baby Boomers will form the largest generation of older citizens in the history of our nation. This aging population will alter our work force, greatly impact healthcare and entitlement programs, and exert pressure on the federal budget. It will also have a profound and changing impact on the church.

Just as each individual has unique needs and wants, so does each generation. While many churches have caught a vision for ministry by, with, and for older adults, it is important to pay particular attention to the similarities and differences of the various midlife and older-adult generations in our churches.

Since no one generation of older adults is the same as another, we make a mistake when we assume that all generations of older adults enjoy the same programs or have exactly the same needs. Many church leaders make the mistake of generalizing about older adults or planning an inflexible program for the present older adults and expecting that program to serve the next older generation without change.

It is helpful for church leaders to realize that in most of our churches there are three different generations of midlife and older adults: GIs, Silents, and Baby Boomers. Each generation has its own unique needs, lifestyles, and beliefs. In fact, it is safe to say that there is no single older-adult population. Rather, there are multiple older-adult populations, and each one is different. Not only do we have three generations from midlife to older adult but there is further complexity within each group: married, widowed, divorced, always single, healthy-active, transitionally impaired, frail-inactive, homebound, institutionalized, dying—and a host of other factors.

In order to help leaders gain a better understanding of each generation, this chapter will explore some of the similarities and differences of the GIs, Silents, and Baby Boomers. With this information, leaders will be better prepared for developing intentional older-adult ministry with the various midlife and older-adult generations.

Although various birth dates are given for each generation, keep in mind that those born at the beginning or end of a particular generation often have some of the characteristics common to two generations. Years are provided to give an approximation for each generation. It is one way social scientists use to gain a greater understanding of various age cohorts, but generational grouping is not an exact science. The information in this chapter is intended to help leaders gain a better understanding of general differences among the various generations.

GI GENERATION

Most of the oldest living Americans are in the GI Generation (also known as the World War II Generation), and they account for 29 million people. They were born between 1905 and 1925, so their attitudes and values were shaped more than anything else by the Great Depression and World War II. They have been a major power in this country and have exerted leadership in every area of business, government, religion, and education. This may be the most affluent elderly generation the nation will see in a long time, as it benefited from an expanding economy and skyrocketing real estate prices. Its members were also the beneficiaries of generous government programs, from the GI Bill to Social Security and Medicare. They are able to enjoy retirement because they have financial security and relatively good health. The GIs are redefining what it means to be old. Instead of being stereotypical frail, impoverished old people, most feel good and live comfortably.

SILENT GENERATION

The next oldest living Americans are members of the Silent Generation (also known as the Swing Generation or Pioneer Generation). Born between 1926 and 1945, this generation was born during the Great Depression and World War II. The number of births declined as the stock market fell in the 1930's, making this generation smaller than the powerful generations that surround it: the GIs and Baby Boomers. This generation is sometimes called the Swing Generation because it swings between the attitudes and lifestyles of the generations on either side. Some members of the Silent Generation share the values and lifestyles of the GIs, while others identify with the Baby Boomers. Sometimes called the Silent Generation, this generation has not had a member elected President of the United States; but it has had several decades of top presidential aides. However, this generation is hardly silent, with such members as Gloria Steinem, Jesse Jackson, and Jerry Falwell. This generation now accounts for 30 million people.

BABY BOOMER GENERATION

Born between 1946 and 1964, the Baby Boomer Generation became the largest generation of Americans up until their time. Today, it numbers 78 million people. Because of their numbers, Baby Boomers have been the focus of attention since their birth. In turn, this massive generation has had an enormous influence on the American economy and culture. For example, when the first Baby Boomers entered public school in the early 1950's, vast national resources were directed to support public education. When they were 18, resources were directed to higher education, which experienced unprecedented expansion. This is the most educated generation in the history of our country. More than one in four (28.5%) has a bachelor's degree. When they entered the work force, resources were diverted to economic development in order to provide jobs and employment. Perhaps this generation is best described as the complete opposite of everything valued by the GI Generation.

Each generation forms distinct attitudes, beliefs, and values during childhood and adolescence. It carries these perspectives throughout life. Generation-specific attitudes become a source of social change as younger generations with new attitudes and values replace older generations.

An Overview

Today's younger older adults hold a variety of attitudes and values that are strikingly different from those held by their elders. For example, they are more liberal toward social issues. From sexuality to authority to women's roles to religion, GIs, Silents, and Baby Boomers stand apart—sometimes far apart. The church is graying not only in terms of the numbers of older adults in the pew but also in terms of clarity related to matters of values, attitudes, beliefs, and lifestyles expressed by each older generation.

This information is important as we plan intentional ministry by, with, and for older adults. Unless we are keenly aware of each generation of older adults, we will fail by attempting to do the same type of ministry with each generation. Just as each individual is unique—with different values, attitudes, and lifestyles—so is each generation.

Who Is Happy?

Although life may seem less exciting as people reach their retirement years, the percentage of adults who indicate that they are "very happy" rises with age. In 2000, 38% of the GI Generation reported that they were very happy, while only 35% of the Baby Boomer Generation and 37% of the Silent Generation indicated the same. On the other hand, 48% of the Baby Boomer Generation felt life was exciting, compared with 36% of the GI Generation.

Roles of Women

Women's roles have changed significantly over the past century. It is no longer the norm for a woman to stay home with the kids while her husband works to support the family. Most women are now in the labor force, and dual family incomes are required for most couples to maintain a middle-class lifestyle. However, the generations have great differences in opinion about this issue. While 72% of the GI Generation think traditional gender roles are best for everyone, only 36% of the Baby Boomer Generation and 52% of the Silent Generation agree.

Authority

Differences concerning unquestioning obedience to authority are prevalent among the generations. For example, when asked what is most important for a child to learn in preparing for life, 37% of the GI Generation stated "to obey" and 36% stated "to think for himself or herself." Fifty-one percent of Baby Boomers stated that it was more important for a child "to think for himself or herself" and only 19% stated "to obey." The Silent Generation fell in the middle, with 46% indicating that it was more important for a child "to think for himself or herself" and 25% choosing "to obey."

FINANCIAL SATISFACTION

In general, people become more satisfied with their financial circumstances as they age. While only 30% of Baby Boomers and 38% of the Silents are "pretty well satisfied" with their financial situation, 43% of the GI Generation are "pretty well satisfied." Few of the oldest adults are still working, so they have relatively low incomes. However, they have Social Security benefits and wealth in the form of homes and investments. They also have lower expenses, since many of them have paid off their mortgages and do not have the expenses associated with working, such as transportation and clothing. They do, however, have higher medical costs.

LEADERSHIP

The following lists identify the types of leaders each generation has great confidence in. They are listed in order of greatest confidence.

GI Generation
• Military
• Medicine
• Scientific community
• Religion
• Education

Silent Generation
• Military (tied with religion)
• Religion
• Medicine (tied with scientific community)
• Scientific community
• Supreme Court (tied with major companies)
• Major companies

Baby Boomer Generation
• Scientific community
• Medicine

- Military
- Supreme Court
- Major companies

The GIs and Silents have far more confidence in leaders of religion than do the Baby Boomers. All three generations indicated that they have much less confidence in leaders of the executive branch of government, organized labor, Congress, television, and the press.

As Americans become better educated, they become less willing to leave decision making to experts. This hands-on attitude is reshaping institutions in fields ranging from religion to education to finance and medicine.

SOCIAL, RELIGIOUS, AND POLITICAL ISSUES

Some of the greatest generational differences of opinion are on social issues. It is not surprising, then, that 25% of Baby Boomers define themselves as liberal, while 18% of GIs do. However, 34% of both generations define themselves as conservative.

Almost half (47%) of the GI Generation believe that premarital sex is "always wrong." However, only 31% of the Silent Generation and 26% of the Baby Boomer Generation believe the same.

Likewise, three-fourths (73%) of the GI Generation believe that sexual relations between two adults of the same sex is "always wrong." But only half (53%) of the Baby Boomer Generation and less than two-thirds (61%) of the Silent Generation believe that homosexual behavior is "always wrong."

Although only 2% of midlife and older adults (GIs, Silents, and Baby Boomers) say they do not believe in God, beliefs about God and the degree of identification with traditional religions vary considerably by age. More than three-fourths (79%) of the GI Generation believe in God without any doubt, while fewer than two-thirds (62%) of both the Silent Generation and the Baby Boomer Generation believe the same.

The generations also have differences concerning regular church attendance. Nationally, almost one of every two (47%) of the GI Generation reports attending religious services at least weekly. However, only 38% of the Silent Generation and 30% of the Baby Boomer Generation attend religious services at least weekly.

The civic-minded GI Generation is most likely to vote and has a higher proportion of registered Democrats. Younger generations more often see themselves as independent, which has eroded party loyalty. Increasingly, voters are choosing candidates who best address their wants and needs, regardless of their political affiliation.

In summary, each generation has well-defined wants and needs. Some of these wants and needs depend on lifestage, while others are created by the events that shape each generation as it ages. Two major concerns—how to provide for the healthcare needs of a growing older population and how to fund Baby Boomers' retirement—will not be easily resolved. An important question for the church is, Once this generation of older adults dies off, what will happen to the church? Since the GI and Silent generations give substantially more money to the church, attend its services, and provide its leadership, what will happen when they are gone? If the church is not intentional in a new ministry with the Baby Boomer Generation, the church will miss reaching a generation of 78 million older adults. And, if the church fails to reach them at midlife and in old age, it will forego a sizeable wealth distribution and miss realizing the wisdom, experience, and faith of this important generation. The church failed to reach the members of this group when they were young. Will the church fail to reach Baby Boomers in old age, too?

Part of the information in this chapter is from American Generations: Who They Are. How They Live. What They Think. *by Susan Mitchell (New Strategist Publications, 2003).*

CHAPTER 3

Why Focus Outreach on Older Adults?

While all people outside the church are in need of our evangelistic concerns, effective outreach communicates the good news in
different ways to different generations. The apostle Paul said, "I have
become all things to all people, that I might by all means save some"
(1 Corinthians 9:22b).

As was stated in preceding chapters, each generation is different in
size and in scope, as well as in the attitudes, values, beliefs, and
lifestyles it holds dear. The purpose of this book is not to help leaders
try to make each generation alike, for that would be impossible. Nor is
it to help leaders design one ministry type that would reach all generations, for that would be nearly impossible. Rather, the purpose of this
book is to help leaders become better stewards of the goal of reaching
all generations of midlife and older adults with the good news of
God's love.

While nearly one of every two adults in the GI Generation attends
religious services at least weekly, and members of the Silent Generation provide greater cash contributions for such things as charitable
(including religious) institutions, the Baby Boomer Generation falls
woefully behind in both church attendance and charitable giving.

So, what happens to the church after the GI and Silent generations are gone? Will it still be in existence? Will the wisdom, experience, and faith of its leadership, which often abounds with older adults, still rest with the elders in the church? Will the church have the finances to keep the doors open, the members to provide vital ministry, and a vision for building God's kingdom here on earth?

Many leaders have written off the Baby Boomer Generation. In fact, some well-meaning, but misguided, leaders have encouraged the church to ignore the Baby Boomers and turn their attention solely to younger generations, including Generation X (also known as Postmoderns) and the Millennials. This move is most unfortunate.

The Baby Boomer Generation continues to exert a numerical influence on our culture and economy and will swell the ranks of people in retirement and older adulthood; therefore, the church cannot afford to ignore so great a generation in its ministry with older adults. It is helpful to remember that Baby Boomers have greatly influenced society at each stage of life. As a result, there is no reason to believe that this influence will cease in old age. In fact, Baby Boomers will probably change most traditional patterns of aging and old age.

Perhaps we need to be reminded at this point that by 2010, 13% of Americans will be 65 years or older, a figure that will continue to rise during the following two decades as 78 million Baby Boomers enter the older age groups. By 2030, more than 20% of Americans will be 65 years or older and will outnumber children and youth under age 18.

With the rise of Baby Boomers in the ranks of older adulthood, the practical family and business focus of today will give way to a more spiritual and exploratory mindset tomorrow as leisure time expands with the aging of the population.

The primary task of the church—making disciples of Jesus Christ—will give way to a clear understanding of our role:
• To reach out and receive all people into the church;
• To help them relate to God through Jesus Christ;
• To nurture them in the Christian faith;
• To support, equip, and send them out to live in the world as Christian disciples.

Older adults, no less than people of other ages and stages of life, are called to be disciples of Jesus Christ. If the church is not active in reaching older adults with the good news of God's love, it fails in its ministry.

Older adults are a worthy, and often receptive, target group on which to focus the ministry of the church. Listed below are a number of reasons it is prudent to focus significant outreach energies on older adults.

God loves older adults. The Scriptures are full of stories demonstrating God's love for older adults. Nowhere in the Bible does it say that God takes away God's blessing when a person reaches age 65. God blesses all life and desires to be in a loving relationship with all God's children, including older adults. If God loves older adults, are we not commanded to love and reach out to older adults, too?

Older adults are closer to eternity. The life expectancy of an average American today is nearly 77 years. If a significant part of our motivation in reaching nonbelievers is to save them from a Christ-less eternity, good outreach strategy would tell us to focus on those who are closest to that eternity.

Older adults are receptive. Because of the transitions and losses in later life, some people are more likely at this time to be open to the ministry of the church. Older adults, when properly introduced to the Christian faith, are open to responding.

Older adults care about others. While Baby Boomers have been described as the Me Generation, research shows that this group is the most likely to volunteer, with one in every three having donated their time. While Baby Boomers volunteered at a higher rate, GIs and Silents devoted the most time to volunteer activities. Not surprising, older volunteers were more likely to volunteer mainly for religious organizations, such as churches. Baby Boomers were more likely to volunteer for educational or youth service organizations first and religious organizations second.

Older adults have more available time. Leaders who are looking for the people power to carry on the ministry of the church will find that older adults have more time to serve than any other age group. Good outreach strategy will focus on empty-nest Baby Boomers and retired GIs and Silents who, once reached, have the time to continue the work of the church.

Older adults are loyal to the church. While the GI and Silent generations are much more dedicated to supporting the goals of an institution to which they belong, Baby Boomers, when given the opportunity to define their own values within the institution, will also support the continuing work of the church. The difference is in degree. GIs and Silents are more likely to be brand loyal, whereas Baby Boomers, who pick and choose what they believe in and what they will support, must be committed to the goals and causes of the institution.

Older adults provide leadership in the church. Church leaders—including teachers, church council members, and committee members—are often older adults. They provide the vision and direction for ministry and reflect the beliefs, attitudes, and ideas of the church. If the church leadership is not growing in faith or experiencing a deeper level of spirituality, the whole church suffers. With an active, growing faith, older adults can provide the necessary leadership for the church to fulfill its mission.

Older adults are geographically more stable. The average American moves every seven years; the average older adult moves every twelve. And most people move when they are younger adults, often to attend school or to seek employment. As a rule, the more rapid the turnover of membership, the more difficult it is for a church to maintain momentum. With a constituency of outward-focused Christian older adults, a church has the best of both worlds: a membership that reaches out to others and stability and longevity. Good outreach strategy will focus on people who will be around for a while.

Older adults give more money to the church. Baby Boomers, Silents, and GIs all provide financial resources for the church. While the church is not in the business of making money, without money it will not long be in the business of making disciples. Because GIs and Silents are more likely to support the institution of the church, they are also more willing to give to that institution; and they have more money to give. The Baby Boomer Generation will amass up to eleven trillion dollars in retirement assets. While the older generations tend to be "institutional givers" (giving to maintain the budget in all necessary areas of the church's ministry), Baby Boomers are more likely to be "issue givers" (giving to selected projects or issues they support). As the Baby Boomers age, the church will need to sell its message to Baby Boomers and adapt a budget that meets their values.

Older adults want to be needed. People of all ages want to feel valued. In our society much of our worth is based on what we do. Many older adults believe they still have something to contribute to society after retirement. And, when given an opportunity, they are providing services and meeting needs. Many older adults look for opportunities for meaningful service and ways to still feel needed. For example, many participate in short-term mission opportunities and in such causes as Habitat for Humanity and Meals on Wheels.

Despite everything listed above, there is considerable ageism in the church. Ageism is behavior that discriminates against, diminishes, and demeans older adults, due solely to their age. While ageism is seldom a conscious choice, a look at the budget, the programming, and the priorities of many churches shows it is often the older adults who get the short end of the stick. The Institute for American Church Growth has found that the ratio of staff who work with youth to staff who work with older adults in churches around the country is approximately 47 to 1. It is this lack of priority in older-adult ministry that is one of the primary reasons that only 1.2% of new Christian converts are over age 60.

We must engage church leaders in a clear understanding that it is not an either/or proposition, meaning that we financially support either children and youth ministry or older-adult ministry. The needs are great among all groups, including older adults. For the church to be effective and faithful to its calling, resources must be distributed according to need. This means that financial, emotional, and spiritual support must be provided not only to children and youth but to all people, including older adults.

How does your church respond to the needs of older adults in your con-gregation? Do you provide funding and staff for older-adult ministry? Is older-adult ministry a priority for your church? Is your church engaged in outreach ministry with older adults in your community? Is the ministry of your older adults valued, recognized, and appreciated?

Much of the information in this chapter is from Riding the Age Wave: A Report on Evange-lizing Today's Older Adults, *a 2002 report on research conducted by the Institute for American Church Growth.*

CHAPTER 4

Older-Adult Ministry in The United Methodist Church

In 2002, the Center on Aging and Older-Adult Ministries of the General Board of Discipleship conducted a survey of older-adult ministries in The United Methodist Church. Approximately 2,000 surveys were mailed to church leaders. Of this number, 338 (17%) were completed and returned.

The church membership size of the respondents varied, but close to two-thirds (62%) of the completed surveys were from churches with 500 or more members:

8	fewer than 50 members
57	50–249 members
61	250–499 members
80	500–999 members
45	1,000–1,499 members
85	1,500 or more members
2	no response

338	Total responses

The survey asked church leaders to respond to the following questions. Their responses are provided.

1. Who carries primary responsibility for older-adult ministry in your local church?

156 of the respondents said laity, which included

   61   Directors or coordinators of older-adult ministries or senior-adult ministries, or chairpersons of older-adult councils or senior-adult councils

   35   Directors/coordinators of adult ministries or chairpersons of adult councils

   21   Directors of Christian education

   15   Chairpersons of witness, evangelism, outreach, and/or nurture committees

   5   Directors of program ministries

   2   Parish nurses

   17   Various other titles (lay leader, parish visitor, ministry team, lay volunteer, and so forth)

124 of the respondents said clergy, which included

   63   Pastors

   42   Associate pastors

   3   Pastors of senior adults

   16   Part-time or retired pastors

46 of the respondents said it was a combination of laity and clergy. Examples included

Parish nurse and minister of visitation

Director of Christian education and director of older-adult ministries

Director of Christian education and minister of senior adults

Pastor and chairperson of adult groups

Pastor, director of Christian education, and director of adult ministries

Pastor and UMW circles

Pastor and parish nurse

Pastor and older-adult council

Associate pastor and director of Christian education

Associate pastor and chairperson of older-adult council

Diaconal minister and pastor

10 of the respondents provided no information.

2 of the respondents said "no one."

2. Do you have a group to plan and carry out your program of older-adult ministry?
   181   Yes
   149   No
     8   No response

3. If you answered "yes" to question 2, what do you call it?
   41   Older-adult council or older-adult ministries
   38   Senior-adult council or senior-adult ministries
   11   Adult council or adult ministries
   91   Other responses, such as
        Education Commission
        Stephen Ministries
        Executive Committee
        Mature Adult Council
        Primetime Council
        Health Ministries
        Caring Ministries
        Nurture Committee

   Examples of names given to older-adult ministries groups include
        SAGES (Senior Adults Growing, Exploring, Serving)
        PEP Council (People Enjoying People)
        Seasoned Citizens
        Primetimers
        XYZ (Xtra Years of Zest)
        Merry Makers
        Zion Zeniors
        Keenagers
        M&M's (Mature & Methodist)
        The Happy Hearts
        Pacesetters
        OWLS (Older, Wiser, Loving Seniors)
        Golden Disciples
        Ageless Senior-Adult Ministries
        Silver Sages
        LIFE (Living in Full Effectiveness)
        RPM (Retired Persons Ministry)
        Funtimers

Zesty Zions
Seniors-on-the-Go
3M's (Merry Mature Methodists)
TNT (Tried 'n True)
Saints Alive
Sizzlin' Seniors
Elderberries
S.E.N.I.O.R.S. Ministry (Spiritual, Enrichment, Nutrition,
	Intergenerational, Outreach, Recreation, and Service)
Live Wires
Happy Timers
The Silvertones
Movers and Shakers
Senior Challengers (challenging the myths of aging)
Young at Heart
METS (Meet, Eat, Travel, Service)

4. If you answered "yes" to question 2, how often do you meet?
   108   Monthly
    53   Quarterly
    10   Twice a year
     8   Twice a month
     2   As needed

5. What is the mission of your older-adult ministry? (Church leaders were
   asked to choose up to 3 options only. Listed below are the top 7 responses.)
   (1) Plan social and fellowship activities for older adults (271)
   (2) Provide outreach and service to older adults (181)
   (3) Provide spiritual growth opportunities for older adults (170)
   (4) Provide educational opportunities for older adults (145)
   (5) Listen to and interpret the needs of older adults to the congregation (94)
   (6) Advocate on behalf of older adults (69)
   (7) Provide evangelistic emphasis for older adults (21)

6. What are some successful activities of your older-adult ministry?
   (Church leaders were invited to choose as many from the list as applied.
   Listed below are the top 10 responses.)
   (1) Fellowship activities (242)
   (2) Visitation of homebound members (232)
   (3) Eatin' and meetin' (229)

(4) Trips and travel opportunities (214)

(5) Bible study and spiritual-growth opportunities (163)

(6) Transportation ministry (103)

(7) Recreational opportunities (102)

(8) Community projects and service (73)

(9) Mission and outreach (71)

(10) Adult day services (16)

7. & 8. What 5 issues do older adults struggle with most in your congregation? Rank them in importance. (Listed below are the top 10 responses.)

(1) Health concerns (325)

(2) Losses (248)

(3) Aging (246)

(4) Living arrangements (160)

(5) Finances (137)

(6) Relationships (83)

(7) Aging parents (79)

(8) Changes in worship (75)

(9) Church accessibility (71)

(10) Social Security and Medicare (70)

9. What issues do you, as a leader, struggle with most in older-adult ministries? (Church leaders were invited to choose up to 3 options. Listed below are the top 8 responses.)

(1) Program ideas (193)

(2) Staffing needs (130)

(3) Budget constraints (118)

(4) Inadequate resources (83)

(5) Diversity issues (64)

(6) Participation and commitment of older-adult leaders (51)

(7) Facilities and accessibility (50)

(8) General attitude of older adults, congregation, and/or pastor concerning older-adult ministries (18)

10. Describe an older-adult ministry that you have seen the need for or dreamed about but have not yet put into practice. (Listed below are the top 15 topics most often mentioned by respondents.)

(1) Transportation ministry

(2) Telephone reassurance ministry

(3) Bible study groups

(4) Intergenerational programs

(5) Adult daycare ministry

(6) Daytime study groups

(7) Meals and financial assistance for older adults in need

(8) Parish nurse ministry

(9) Creating an atmosphere of respect for older adults

(10) Shepherd's Center

(11) Community ministry

(12) Visitation ministry

(13) Handyman ministry

(14) Drama and music ministry

(15) Grandparenting ministry

11. What resources are needed to help you be a more effective leader of older-adult ministries? (Listed below are the top 6 responses.)

(1) Training

(2) How to motivate older adults

(3) How to be an effective leader of older-adult ministries

(4) How to organize an older-adult ministry

(5) Program/ministry ideas

(6) General resource information

From responses provided by church leaders, we can get a fair glimpse of older-adult ministries in The United Methodist Church. For example, the church is almost evenly divided between calling this ministry older-adult ministries or senior-adult ministries. Although the church has used the term older-adult ministry for many years, some churches prefer naming it senior-adult ministry. Many churches prefer not to use either name but rather to combine this ministry with some other existing body, such as the education commission, nurture committee, or Stephen Ministries.

The majority of older-adult ministry leaders are laity. However, a number of clergy also carry primary responsibility for this important ministry.

The mission of older-adult ministry in most of our churches appears to be planning social and fellowship activities for older adults, while providing outreach and service and providing spiritual growth opportunities take a distant second and third place. And fewer than one of every sixteen churches identifies an important mission in providing an evangelistic emphasis for older adults.

The major concern of most older adults in our churches relates to health concerns, followed closely by losses and aging issues. If this is the case, congregations need to develop wellness and health ministries and to provide support networks for grief and loss.

It is important to remember that many of the problems of old age are not due to aging but to improper care of the body over a lifetime. Aging is a lifestyle issue. The amount of exercise people engage in, the way people handle stress, the foods they eat, and a host of other factors all contribute to the well-being of older adults.

A further look at this survey reveals that church leaders are concerned about program ideas. They are looking for ways to motivate, engage, and empower older adults. Part of their frustration is due to the lack of staffing and to budget constraints. Leaders want quality training opportunities, useful resources, and help with being effective leaders of older adults. This book is intended to help leaders maximize their potential and increase their knowledge for effective and intentional ministry by, with, and for older adults.

CHAPTER 5

S.E.N.I.O.R.S.:
A Comprehensive
Older-Adult Ministry

Older adults are often overlooked in our society. Age discrimination is not a new phenomenon, but it has become a more visible problem with our aging population. Age discrimination is complex and occurs in a variety of ways. One common situation involves a person who loses employment in the middle and later years and finds it difficult to secure other employment. A second common situation involves those who no longer receive training opportunities, are not promoted to a higher-level position, or are discharged simply for being old.

The United Methodist Church has a policy that all ordained clergy must retire at 70 years of age (if retirement has not already happened at an earlier age). With our growing shortage of pastors, retired pastors may be invited to lead congregations; but they are often given a smaller salary and fewer benefits. With people living longer and healthier today than ever before, many pastors in their 70s and 80s may have more experience, energy, and wisdom for ministry than their junior colleagues have. The United Methodist Committee on Older-Adult Ministries believes that age alone should not be the qualifier for such decisions about retirement. Rather, retooling and retraining opportunities should be provided continuously for all pastors in this fast-paced and changing world. The Committee on Older-Adult Ministries has proposed legislation to General Conference calling for the removal of mandatory retirement at age 70 for clergy.

Unfortunately, many in our society tend to view older adults as helpless victims of neglect and indifference. Some younger people perceive the elderly not as victims but as victimizers, exploiters of youth because they selfishly cling to their jobs and to a disproportionate share of wealth, power, and resources. Although these two perceptions seem diametrically opposed, they may reflect the same anxiety: Old age is a time to be feared by young and old alike.

Fears related to healthcare costs, Social Security solvency, Medicare expenses, social services, and so forth create a scenario of denial, burden, or impending crisis in society. Old age is viewed as immoral, demeaning, unnatural, morbid, or diseased. Older adults become objects of jokes and ridicule or are simply ignored. The rich resources older adults can provide—the talent and wisdom gained only with age—are often not being used to their fullest extent.

Since our beginning, The United Methodist Church (including its former predecessor bodies: United Brethren in Christ; Evangelical Association; Methodist Episcopal; Methodist Episcopal, South; and Methodist Protestant) has been strongly committed to evangelism and nurture. We have always opened our arms to all people, young and old alike. As Christians, we look at this situation of the elderly through eyes of faith. The gospel of Jesus Christ is our foundation, and that gospel is an offer of life abundance to all. With the growing numbers of older adults in our midst, the church must be vigilant and intentional in its ministry with the elderly. The church must address the needs and use the skills of older adults in our congregations.

In addition, leaders in the church should encourage older adults to take charge of their own lives, as far as they are able to assume responsibility for the stewardship of their time, health, possessions, and social relations. Older adults should be given responsibility for developing, implementing, and coordinating programs of ministry by, with, and for older adults, rather than having such programs planned and produced by others for them.

Churches genuinely concerned about a rich and abundant life for all people will develop a vital ministry with older adults. One important ministry model for congregations seeking to develop a comprehensive older-adult ministry is the S.E.N.I.O.R.S. model. This ministry model is effective for ministry in small-membership to large-membership churches. Composed of seven vital components, the S.E.N.I.O.R.S. ministry model is both an intentional and a wholistic approach to older-adult ministry. The seven components are spiritual, enrichment, nutrition and fitness, intergenerational, outreach, recreation, and service.

SPIRITUAL

Naturally, the church plays a vital role in the spiritual well-being of people of all ages. For older adults, spiritual guidance is made available through worship, pastoral care, Bible study, prayer groups, and support networks that enable people to cope with life's situations and to find meaning and purpose for their lives.

God has much to say in Scripture about aging, which is a gift from God and has a purpose. In Job, the question is asked, "Is wisdom with the aged, and understanding in length of days?" (12:12). An answer is given in Proverbs, "Gray hair is a crown of glory; it is gained in a righteous life" (16:31).

Second Corinthians 4:16-18 reminds us that what is important in life is far deeper than what we see: gray hair, wrinkles, and hearing aids. What is important is what we are inside, rather than how we look. Our inner nature is renewed each day. Gray hair, wrinkles, and hearing aids do not mean older adults are retired from faithfulness. We are called to be faithful regardless of age. God does not withhold or take away God's blessing when people grow older. Helping older adults remember and experience God's love in the face of adversity, grief, and loss is important for their spiritual well-being.

Through worship, the longing, aspirations, frustrations, failures, cares, and losses experienced in the later years will be articulated in prayers, hymns, and sermons. The milestones passed and goals achieved will be celebrated. Rituals should be created to support older adults in making the transitions common to the later years, such as dealing with change, separation, and new commitments.

For example, if Martha is moving from her home of forty years, instead of simply announcing in the weekly church bulletin or newsletter that she is moving and printing her new address, suppose the church provided the following ritual. Along with several of Martha's friends or acquaintances, a group visits Martha in her home. When gathered in the living room or around the kitchen table, they sing hymns, read Scripture, offer prayers, and receive Holy Communion. They then give God thanks for the many years Martha has lived in her home. If possible, Martha then leads her guests through her house. In each room, she is invited to tell her memories of joy and sorrow. After Martha has moved to her new place of residence, her friends could gather with her again. They could sing hymns, read Scripture, offer prayers, and break bread together. Then they could ask that God's blessing be with Martha in her new home. Think of the difference this ritual could make in Martha's life, as well as in the lives of her friends and of the entire congregation. This is just one of the many types of rituals congregations can develop for the spiritual well-being of older adults.

As church leaders, we are encouraged to help older adults grow older faithfully and with God's grace. Since spiritual renewal is essential to life fulfillment, the church plays a vital role in helping older adults attain this goal. Providing opportunities for the continuing spiritual growth of older adults is important not only for the individual and the church but also for the transformation of the world.

ENRICHMENT

Personal enrichment is important for the well-being of older adults. In a fast-paced and changing society, older adults need opportunities to continue the lifelong process of learning and growing.

Classes, courses, forums, and discussion groups can be planned to enable older adults to anticipate and prepare for possible life transitions. Continuing education opportunities can help older adults increase their skills in communication, in human relations, in problem solving, and in decision making. Seminars can help older adults understand the grief process and the resources that can be called on in time of need.

When the congregation is a learning community—providing a positive climate for learning and support for change—older adults are assured of their ability to learn new things, are able to reflect on and to tell about their memories, and are encouraged to be creative.

Opportunities for expanding horizons through travel, lectures, mission trips, and conversations with people from other places, races, and ethnic groups are all important for the personal enrichment of older adults.

Becoming familiar with new technology is also vital for older adults. For example, your congregation could develop a computer lab for older adults with the help of knowledgeable techies from your congregation. These techies are often youth or other young people who might enjoy teaching older adults about computers and the Internet. However, do not overlook some of your older members who may have vast experience with computers and the Internet and would enjoy helping others.

Congregations should assist older adults in discovering their vocation within the context of their situations, recruit them for ministry in the church and in the community, and support them in their ministry through nurture and training.

NUTRITION AND FITNESS

As we grow older, our recuperative powers diminish. Thus, we accumulate a distressing collection of chronic incurable conditions. Some of these are no more than a minor nuisance, and we adapt as best we can. When adaptation is not possible, we learn to tolerate the nuisance. Some conditions are more serious, involving severe disability and persistent pain, and may eventually become life threatening.

As we age, we are also at risk for various acute conditions (such as influenza and pneumonia), which are more serious threats to the health of elderly people than to younger people. And, as we age, there are more incidents of cancer and heart disease. Living longer would not matter if the extra years of life were predominantly healthy, but it would matter if the extra years were ones of disability, pain, and increasing dependence on others.

Fortunately, the great majority of older adults live in community, are cognitively intact, and are fully independent in their daily activities. Those who remain active may be individuals who exercise, eat nutritious foods, and have a positive psychological view of life.

The church plays an important role in providing for the physical well-being of older adults. From providing meals to exercise classes to adult day services, churches are beginning to see the correlation between nutrition and physical fitness and successful aging.

Elements that are important to staying healthy as one grows older—eating nutritious foods, having a positive outlook on life, exercising regularly, keeping stress to a minimum, and getting routine physical exams—can be provided by caring congregations. By establishing a parish nurse ministry or a congregational wellness program, for example, churches can assist older adults in maintaining a reasonable degree of independence.

Creating opportunities for older adults to engage in low-impact exercise, to eat nutritious meals, and to have support networks can go a long way in helping older adults remain active and vital in the later years.

INTERGENERATIONAL

People of all ages need others. It is better to speak of each person being interdependent rather than being either independent or dependent. We need one another, and this need expresses itself in healthy relationships as nurturing and caring opportunities.

Erik Erikson described such a need for older adults as "generativity," or the desire to help benefit future generations. In later years, according to Erikson, older adults have the desire to impart knowledge, wisdom, and experience for the benefit of succeeding generations. The church, as an institution, provides people of all ages with the opportunity to intermingle and learn from one another. It is a place where older adults can share their faith and impart their wisdom, if given the opportunity.

While it is recognized that there is a need and a place for age-graded or group-oriented programs, it is also important that churches provide opportunities for people of various ages as well as diverse backgrounds and social interests to be together. No one generation or group of people holds all knowledge, faith, or wisdom. Old and young alike should be encouraged to work together, to study together, and to play together while learning from one another.

Older adults should be encouraged to serve as volunteers in programs serving other age groups, such as tutoring children, being a foster grandparent, or relating either to single-parent families or to families who have children with handicapping conditions. Older adults can teach children in the church school or vacation Bible school programs. Older adults can volunteer their services for before-school or after-school activities and can mentor children involved in confirmation classes or in Scouting and other civic youth service programs.

Younger people may be involved in volunteer service for older adults, such as delivering Meals on Wheels, providing transportation, helping with minor home repairs and maintenance, and running errands.

Younger and older people may be teamed up together to provide particular ministries, such as working to clean up the environment, visiting people who are homebound, participating in short-term mission projects, attending a weekend spiritual retreat, and securing changes in social policies or institutional practices.

OUTREACH

A program of outreach and evangelism seeks to include all the older adults in its fellowship, recognizing that many older adults do not have an active relationship with any congregation. Older adults should feel welcomed rather than ignored, rejected, humiliated, or dehumanized when they come to participate in any programs of the church.

Church leaders should be careful of their language. For example, saying that the church is family-oriented may make single adults and people who are widowed or divorced feel uncomfortable or unwelcome. Likewise, joking about the age of older adults, their appearance (baldness), or their plans for retirement may be done with good intentions; but it could cause hurt feelings.

In addition, keep information about older adults up-to-date in a central file or database so that no one is forgotten or overlooked and each person's resources are known. Sometimes called a talent and needs inventory, it provides church leaders with important information about the older adults in the community.

All facilities within the church building or within the places where programs are held should be accessible to those with limiting or disabling conditions. Install ramps, elevators, and ground-level entrances. Likewise, provide hearing aids or amplified speech for people who have impaired hearing. Make available large-print Bibles, hymnals, worship bulletins, and devotional booklets for those with diminished sight.

Provide opportunities for those who are homebound to join with others in worship or fellowship. This could include broadcasting or taping worship services for delivery to the home and holding worship services, Bible studies, and meetings in the home.

While older adults, especially those who are lonely, should be visited regularly, those undergoing stress as a result of loss or illness should receive continuing support and pastoral care as needed. In addition, older adults who are new in the community should be adopted by members of the congregation who can assist in their assimilation into the life of the congregation and support them in their Christian commitment.

Finally, every effort should be made to remove all physical, psychological, economic, and social obstacles that make it difficult for older adults to participate in the life and ministry of the congregation.

RECREATION

Older adults can literally think themselves into the grave by feeling bad about getting old. Attitude is an important index in prolonging life expectancy. Studies have shown that older adults who have had more positive views about aging live an average 7.6 years longer than those who have had negative ones.

Older adults need creative self-expression, opportunities to develop and maintain self-confidence, a sense of humor, and a capacity for play. As a result, the need for play, recreation, and fellowship is no less great for older adults than it is for people of all ages. Recreation and play add an extra measure of zest to the lives of aging people, enhancing both physical and mental well-being.

According to George Vaillant, in his book *Aging Well,* learning to play again is one of the leading factors in having a rewarding retirement. He writes that, according to a fifty-year longitudinal study, there are four factors to having a rewarding retirement:

• replacing work mates with another social network;
• rediscovering how to play;
• making time for creativity;
• continuing lifelong learning.

SERVICE

The mission of the church is to make disciples of Jesus Christ. As disciples, older adults are called to a ministry of service. Unfortunately, we often hear older adults say, "I have done my part," or "It is time to get others [younger people?] involved," or "I'm too old." While we always want to encourage and equip leaders of all ages, we certainly do not want the faith, wisdom, and experience that often abound in older adults to be lost or underutilized.

Since it is important for older adults to maintain a sense of self-worth and to feel useful and needed, involving them in service opportunities is vital to their well-being. Encouraging, equipping, and supporting older adults in their ministry is an important task of congregations.

Chapter 6 discusses issues of motivating older adults. Chapter 7 provides greater detail concerning the various ways both congregations and older adults can serve the needs of older adults.

Motivation
and Older Adults

How can we motivate older adults for service? Why do some older adults never seem to stop serving, while others can never seem to start? Many older adults find new ways of serving others, their communities, and their world. Some say that they have done their work, so it is now time for others to take over.

It is helpful to remember that some older adults have reached their limit. They have worked themselves into exhaustion and are not able to carry on in ministry. Having engaged in ministry for many years, they are physically, emotionally, or even spiritually weary. Some may simply need time to rest and to reflect, to retool, and to reenergize their bodies, minds, and spirits. Others no longer have the strength, the desire, or the passion for ministry. Thankfully, this is not true for everyone.

Most older adults want to feel needed and useful, to know that their lives have meaning and purpose. They want to continue to be involved fully in life and in ministry. Often, involvement is just a matter of motivation. One question I often hear from leaders is, "How can I motivate older adults?"

First, we must recognize that older adults are already motivated to do what they are already doing. It may be sitting in a rocking chair and watching television all day. It may be playing eighteen holes of golf three days a week or learning more about computers and the Internet. It may be caring for a spouse with Alzheimer's disease or raising grandchildren in the absence of their parents. It may be tutoring children or participating in a short-term mission trip. It may be reading the Bible and meditating on the Word of God or delivering meals to residents in the community who are homebound. For whatever reason, adults are motivated to be doing what they are already doing.

Second, it is possible that older adults do not know what they want to do or what they can do. Many church leaders ask older adults to perform specific tasks, but they rarely invite older adults to be in ministry. As a result, older adults have an expectation that the church is supposed to be doing something for them. And, while we invite young people to participate in spiritual gifts discovery workshops, we may never think to invite older adults. We may believe older adults are too old to participate, already have the information, or are not interested in participating. How do we know, unless we ask?

Third, it is important that we accept the fact that older adults may be called to a different ministry. While we may believe there is an important task that Mildred or Tom can do, they may hear God speaking to them differently. For example, Mildred may sincerely want to stop teaching a children's Sunday school class. Although she accepted the position only for the summer when her children were quite young, she has faithfully stayed in that position for the past fifty years. Instead of trying to encourage Mildred to stay in that position, church leaders would do well to help Mildred capture a new vision for ministry. Likewise, Tom might have helped the Boy Scouts on their camping trips for many years; however, since his heart attack and recent bypass surgery, he no longer feels comfortable in wilderness settings. While the Boy Scouts may need a leader, Tom is in search of a new ministry.

Fourth, older adults might not feel adequate in doing the job, since information and training might not be provided. They may feel insecure about performing a task for which they have neither experience nor training. Furthermore, they may be fearful that they will not do the job correctly or, worse yet, embarrass themselves. Feelings of inadequacy and uncertainty are real emotions for older adults. Church leaders would do well to help alleviate fears by providing training opportunities and by creating win-win situations. Providing a coach, mentor, or coworker to help an older adult can be a positive experience for gaining knowledge and alleviating fears.

Fifth, a major problem that older adults face is related neither to health nor to finances. Rather, it is a loss of vision. When older adults no longer feel useful or no longer have a sense of purpose, they are without a dream or vision for life. You have probably heard an older adult say, "I don't know why God keeps me here." What this older person is saying is, "I no longer have a vision for living." It is crucial for church leaders to help older adults capture a new dream, to help them experience a new vision for ministry. When older adults have a vision for ministry, they also have passion, motivation, and creativity.

Sixth, some older adults get turned off just by the title older adult or senior adult. We must acknowledge that many older adults do not like to be called older, senior, senior citizen, or elderly. Any program that identifies itself as an older-adult ministry or senior-adult ministry creates negative feelings among some older adults. If these negative feelings persist, older adults may not participate in that ministry.

Adults who voice the strongest opposition to seeing themselves as older adults or senior adults are usually younger older adults. This is natural because they really do not see themselves as older and do not feel old. They are active, still working, and see themselves as young or middle-age adults. They recognize that physical changes are taking place, that their energy level is lessening, or that their hair is thinning or turning gray; but they are not old.

Baby Boomers in particular have railed against being described as older adults. In a study done by the Office of Adult Ministries of the General Board of Discipleship in 1999, Baby Boomers were asked to identify what they wanted to be called when they were in their retirement years. It was clear from their responses that Baby Boomers did not want to be identified as older adults or senior adults. Rather, Baby Boomers preferred to be identified in the retirement years as adults or mature adults. Needless to say, churches that are involved in older-adult or senior-adult ministry will have a difficult time reaching Baby Boomers.

So, what are leaders to do? Some churches have little or no problem identifying their ministry with older adults as an older-adult or senior-adult ministry. That is evident from our research reported in Chapter 4. Leaders in churches that have difficulty can do the following:
• Hold seminars on myths and realities of aging.
• Conduct workshops on the positive and negative aspects of growing older.
• Include positive images of older adults in sermon illustrations, stories, and articles.
• Be careful in the use of language so that older adults feel included, not left out, ignored, or unwanted.
• Design a comprehensive ministry by, with, and for older adults.

- Be intentional in older-adult ministry about recognizing, valuing, and respecting the gifts and lives of older adults.
- Provide opportunities for intergenerational sharing and learning.
- Call ministry by a name other than older or senior. For example, some churches choose a name like Live Wires, XYZ (Xtra Years of Zest), or Mature Methodists to identify their ministry with older adults. For other possibilities, see the answers to survey question 3, on pages 31–32.

Finally, in addition to the ideas suggested above, there are some specific ways you can help encourage and motivate older adults. Listed below are fifteen easy, yet effective, ways of inviting and involving older adults in ministry.

1. Develop a shared vision for ministry with older adults. Tell about your vision as a church leader and invite older adults to tell their vision. Have a meeting of the minds.
2. Accept older adults for who they are, individual and unique children of God. Leaders must remember that they cannot force their ideals, their values, or even their ministry goals on others.
3. Involve older adults in the decision-making process. Ask them what they think. Older adults have lots of experience and knowledge to contribute.
4. Know the needs and talents of older adults. Do not try to fit a round peg into a square hole. Be certain you know the capabilities and needs of older adults in order to match abilities with tasks.
5. Support older adults' spiritual gifts. Encourage them to discover their spiritual gifts; then match your ministry needs with their gifts.
6. Personally invite older adults to become active participants in ministry. Help them integrate their faith in their daily life.
7. Accommodate personal needs and problems and make your building accessible. Install ramps, railings, hearing aid devices, accessible restrooms, wheelchair lifts, and handicapped parking spaces. Provide large-print bulletins, Bibles, hymnals, and songbooks.
8. Say thank you and give recognition freely. Find ways to express your appreciation (a postcard or note, an e-mail message, a recognition banquet, a recognition worship service) for the ministry of older adults. Older adults need incentives to participate in ministry.
9. Keep older adults informed. Use regular newsletters to make them feel included and important. Post information on an older-adult ministries bulletin board in an area of the church where older adults congregate. Develop an older-adult ministries website.

10. Phone or stop by for a visit. Make sure older adults know how important they are to the ministry of the church. Good workers deserve compliments.
11. Never forget a birthday or anniversary. Cards mean a lot to older adults.
12. Greet older adults with a smile. It may seem trivial, but greeting older adults with a warm welcome and a big smile helps establish a positive tone for ministry.
13. Involve older adults in learning opportunities. Invite them to learn about new ideas and resources for ministry. Older adults want to continue learning. Your willingness to include them in training opportunities says that you value them and their ministry.
14. Provide on-the-job training. We often ask people to provide a particular ministry, but we seldom prepare them adequately for the task. Conduct training sessions so that older adults feel more comfortable performing the assigned task or ministry.
15. Engage older adults in prayer and Bible study. Allow God's Word to excite and invite older adults into mature faith and discipleship. As a result, God will place on their hearts opportunities to be involved in ministry.

CHAPTER 7

Models for Older-Adult Ministry

As you begin developing an intentional ministry by, with, and for older adults, keep in mind two important facts. First, every older adult is a unique individual, and no two older adults are exactly alike. As people live longer, their experiences due to education, socio-economic factors, health conditions, life and work opportunities, and a host of other influences create uniqueness and individuality. You may look at Martha, who is not related to you, and see your grandmother. Yet, Martha is not your grandmother. She may have entirely different needs and abilities than your grandmother had. She may resemble her only in features or in mannerisms. If you presuppose that Martha has ideals, values, and desires like your grandmother's, you do an injustice to Martha, do harm to yourself, and fail in your ministry.

Second, it is important to remember that no model for older-adult ministry will work exactly the same way in two different settings. You may believe that you can successfully replicate a particular ministry in your setting because it works well in another church. People, needs, and environments are different; therefore, ministry models may not work the same in two different churches. While you may use an idea for ministry that is working well in another setting, you may not be able to implement the ministry with the same exact detail in your own church, no matter how hard you try. However, you may be able to implement the ministry in a similar form suitable for the needs of your congregation. In order to design an intentional ministry by, with, and for older adults, church leaders should identify the needs of older adults in their setting, develop and implement a program suitable to meet those needs, and then evaluate the effectiveness of such a ministry.

Listed below are selected ministry ideas that may be valuable and helpful for ministry with older adults in your church.

- **Adult Children Caring for Aging Parents:** Today, the number of older adults caring for their aging parents is a growing phenomenon. Churches can create opportunities for support, fellowship, and learning for these caregivers.

- **Adult Day Service:** Older adults can provide a safe place during the day for people needing special attention while their family members are at work.

- **Advertising in the Local Theater and Senior Citizen Center:** Older-adult ministry is advertised in the local theater, senior citizen center, restaurants, and other places older adults congregate so that older adults in the community know about the church's ministry.

- **Annual Older-Adult Picnic:** Older adults from the church and community participate in a summer picnic. Food (meat and drink), entertainment, and games are provided. Picnic goers are asked to bring a side dish or dessert.

- **Body Recall:** This is a program of physical fitness specifically designed for older adults (see page 69).

- **Caregiving:** Older adults provide direct care for people having difficulty with activities of daily living: walking, bathing, dressing, getting to/from bed, going outdoors, preparing meals.

- **Childcare Ministry:** Older adults provide childcare services while parents are at work: before-school or after-school programs, a Mother's Day Out program, or a special Parent's Night Out program.

- **Companion Services:** Older adults escort and help other older adults when they go to the doctor, dentist, pharmacy, grocery store, and so forth.

- **Congregational Health Ministry:** This is a wholistic approach to congregational health and wellness ministries by the General Board of Global Ministries (see page 62).

- **Eucharistic Ministers:** After the elements have been blessed and consecrated by the pastor, older adults serve as Eucharistic ministers and take the sacrament of Holy Communion to people who are homebound and to others with special needs. In addition to serving the bread and cup, they use appropriate ritual, prayers, and Scripture.

- **Field Trips:** Older adults participate in trips that are educational, recreational, mission study, or work mission. Usually, field trips take only a day, although they sometimes take a weekend.

- **Fine Arts Program:** Older adults take part in drama, plays, music, choir, arts and crafts, and other hobbies. They have special presentations of plays and choir performances for the church and the general public.

- **Fitness and Nutrition:** Older adults participate in low-impact aerobics classes or some other form of exercise designed for older adults. They take classes about cooking for one and nutritious meal preparation.

- **Flowers for Those Who Are Homebound or Hospitalized:** Following the worship service, older adults deliver the church flowers to members who are homebound or hospitalized.

- **Foster Grandparents:** Older adults serve as foster grandparents for children and youth who have few or no extended family members living in the community.

- **Game Day:** Once a week or monthly, a game day for older adults is held. Card games, board games, and games of challenge to help mental stimulation are particularly helpful.

- **Grief and Loss Support Groups:** Older adults participate in support groups dealing with grief and loss. These may include a widow/widower support group, a divorce support group, a stroke support group, or other support groups for people coping with grief and loss issues.

- **Helping Hands:** Older adults maintain a church food pantry and clothing closet. They collect food and clothing from church members and then make them available to people in need.

- **Homebound Sunday School Participation:** Class members who are homebound participate in Sunday school by use of a speakerphone, which is centrally located in the classroom. The members who are homebound dial in, listen, and respond along with the other adults present in the class.

- **Homebound Worship Participation:** Members who are homebound read Scripture, offer morning prayer, or participate in other liturgical acts by using a telephone hooked up to the church sound system.

- **Home Maintenance and Minor Repair:** Older adults with skills help others by painting, changing light bulbs, mowing lawns, providing home chore services, doing carpentry, and fixing plumbing problems.

- **House Sharing:** Older adults share housing with college students in exchange for chore service, minor home repair, cooking, or laundry. The rent is free or greatly reduced for the students in exchange for services provided to older adults.

- **Intergenerational Retreat:** Older adults and youth participate in a retreat together, which includes games, meals, Bible study, and sharing. Recreation and fellowship opportunities are encouraged.

- **Involve Other Churches:** Many small-membership congregations have limited staff and financial resources, making it difficult to provide for needed ministries. Two or more churches may find that joining forces opens up new possibilities for ministry.

- **Kitchen Band:** Older adults make musical instruments from common materials found around the house and play them at special functions at nursing homes (and other long-term healthcare settings), retirement communities, and church.

- **Latchkey Kid Ministry:** Older adults provide a daily after-school program for children until their parents get home from work. The ministry includes tutoring and mentoring the children.

- **Life Review:** Older adults participate in life review and reminiscence classes, where they talk about their life journey and faith stories. Information and reflection is recorded in journals or on video or cassette tape.

- **Living History:** Older adults talk about experiences of their life in the church or in the community. Their stories are put on tape (video and/or audio) and/or in writing and repeated orally in worship, in a Sunday school class, or at an intergenerational program.

- **Lunch Partners:** Older adults make weekly visits to members of the church or community who are homebound. They join in fellowship and share a lunch that has been prepared and delivered or a brown-bag lunch that they have brought.

• **Marriage Enrichment:** Older married couples lead and participate in marriage enrichment programs. Older couples serve as mentors for young married couples or continue to learn new communication techniques and interpersonal relationship skills to grow a happy marriage during the retirement years. For contact information about various marriage enrichment-type ministries, see pages 68 and 71.

• **Meal Delivery:** Older adults prepare and deliver meals for people who are temporarily homebound or who have recently been hospitalized. Many churches also participate in the Meals on Wheels program.

• **Meals:** Many churches hold a weekly or monthly luncheon for older adults. The meal may be catered by an outside business or by church members. In many cases, older adults prepare the meal themselves, usually in the form of a covered dish lunch. Often, a program of entertainment, a Bible study, or a guest speaker follows the meal.

• **Mentoring:** Older adults serve as mentors for children, youth, and adults. Two excellent opportunities include mentoring youth in the confirmation class and mentoring new church members.

• **Multigenerational Study Groups:** Children, youth, and adults study and learn together. Topics might include Bible study and/or current events (comparative religion, peace and justice issues, community concerns, or computer classes).

• **Newsletter:** Some churches have created a newsletter for the older adults in the congregation. Older adults are invited to submit articles, poetry, prayers, and devotional materials. The newsletter includes information relevant to the needs of older adults, highlights of various older-adult ministries, recognition of ministry of specific older adults, and announcements about meetings, activities, and events.

• **NOMADS:** Older adults with recreational vehicles travel around the country providing service and ministry for special projects (see pages 63–64).

• **Nursing Home Sunday School Class:** On a regular basis, older adults participate in a Sunday school class in nursing homes and assisted-living settings. Large-print curriculum resources, audio tapes, and video cassettes provide opportunities for residents to grow in Christian faith and to experience God's love.

- **Nursing Home VBS:** For one week each year, older adults lead a daily vacation Bible school for residents in nursing homes and in assisted-living settings. The support and cooperation of the activities and social service departments in the nursing homes and assisted-living settings are enlisted.

- **Older-Adult Choir:** Older adults form a choir to sing at church, nursing homes, retirement communities, and the homes of people who are home-bound. These choirs give special performances and participate in such activities as Christmas caroling within the community.

- **Outreach and Evangelism:** Older adults are trained and encouraged to reach out to other older adults who need spiritual support and new life in Jesus Christ. Older adults invite others to church and Sunday school or to other church-related events. These older adults distribute flyers and brochures about the church and its ministries.

- **Parish Nurse Ministry:** Churches may employ or enlist a volunteer parish nurse to be on the staff of the church to monitor the health of the older adults. This position, whether paid or volunteer, may be a full-time or part-time service. Information and education related to the health needs of older adults are provided through seminars, workshops, and personal consultations. (For more information on parish nurse ministry, see the General Board of Global Ministries' "Health and Welfare Ministries" and "Health Ministries Association," on pages 62 and 70.)

- **Primetimers:** A new ministry of the General Board of Global Ministries, Primetimers is a program of learning, service, and faith sharing for mature adults (see pages 63–64). Older adults participate in an Elderhostel-type learning program combined with a Volunteer in Mission-type service opportunity.

- **Recognition Banquet:** The congregation sponsors a dinner or banquet in recognition of the life and faithful service of older adults. The meal is catered or prepared and served by young families of the church. The presentation of outstanding service awards is the high point of the banquet.

- **Recognition Service:** During a Sunday in May (Older-Adult Month) or on the second Sunday in September (Grandparents Day), a special worship service is held on Sunday morning to honor the faith, wisdom, ministry, and service of older adults. The Administration on Aging (see page 73) provides a theme each year for Older-Adult Month.

- **Respite Care Ministry:** Older adults provide respite for people serving as primary caregivers for loved ones. Older adults visit with the person needing care so that the primary care provider can get out of the house to go to the store, church, doctor, or movie theater.

- **Ritual for Older Adults Who Move From Their Homes:** A small group of older adults visits with a person who is moving from a home to a long-term healthcare facility. They pray, read Scripture, sing, receive Holy Communion, and speak words of remembrance and thanksgiving for the years spent in the home. They follow up with a similar ritual in the new residence.

- **Senior Bulletin Board:** A large bulletin board is placed in a location in the church where older adults congregate. Posted on the board are announcements about events, trips and travel opportunities, help wanted ads, and photos of recent activities and events.

- **Senior Devotional Booklet:** Older adults compile a devotional book of prayers, stories, Scripture, and poems for congregational use during the season of Advent and/or Lent.

- **S.E.N.I.O.R.S. Ministry:** Congregations involve older adults in a comprehensive and intentional ministry that includes programs related to spirituality, enrichment, nutrition and fitness, intergenerational, outreach, recreation, and service opportunities. For more information about S.E.N.I.O.R.S. ministry, see Chapter 5 (pages 37–44).

- **Senior Yearbook:** Older adults create an annual yearbook that includes photos and stories related to activities, travel, and mission trips performed by the older-adult group.

- **Shepherd's Center:** Older adults participate in an ecumenical ministry meeting the needs of older adults. The four components of this ministry include maintenance, enrichment, reorganization, and celebration. For contact information, see pages 71–72.

- **Short-Term Mission Service:** Older adults participate in short-term mission projects, which may be in the community or around the world (Habitat for Humanity, Volunteers in Mission, or a local mission project).

- **Stephen Ministries:** Older adults visit children, youth, and adults who are ill, homebound, institutionalized, or have other needs. For contact information about Stephen Ministries, see page 72.

- **Sunday Afternoon Worship for People Who Are Homebound:** Monthly, quarterly, or biannually, a Sunday afternoon worship service (including Holy Communion) is conducted in the church sanctuary for members who are homebound. Family members are asked to provide transportation, or special travel arrangements are made. The church sanctuary is decorated for the season of the year. The choir is invited to sing a familiar anthem, a brief meditation is given, and the sacrament of Holy Communion is administered. The length of service is kept to a maximum of thirty to forty minutes.

- **Sweetheart and Others Dinner:** Valentine's Day provides an opportunity for older couples and others to enjoy a delicious dinner and dancing or special entertainment. The meal is catered or prepared and served by young families of the church. The music is varied and of special interest to the generations in attendance.

- **Teaching and Leading:** Older adults are encouraged to teach study groups and Sunday school classes, to lead in worship, and to hold meaningful leadership positions in the church.

- **Telephone Reassurance:** Older adults make daily phone calls to members who are homebound. Information concerning particular needs and assistance is given to appropriate church personnel. Phone calls are made at the same time each day, unless previously instructed otherwise.

- **Travel Opportunities:** Older adults take trips and travel excursions for pleasure and learning. These trips might be local one-day bus trips or weekend regional trips. Some churches may even sponsor travel opportunities to the Holy Land or somewhere else in the world.

- **Visitation Ministry:** Older adults visit other older adults who are homebound, lonely, hospitalized, institutionalized, or dying. They then give information concerning particular needs and assistance to appropriate church personnel.

- **Weekday Bible Study:** Older adults in the church and community participate in a weekday Bible study. The group may study a particular book of the Bible or engage in a specialized program, such as DISCIPLE Bible study. Refreshments, a time for sharing joys and concerns, hymn singing, and prayers are included.

CHAPTER 8

Selected Resource Directory

As seen in the previous chapters in this book, what has become increasingly clear concerning older adults is their differences not just in numbers but in vitality and outlook. With the growing numbers of older adults in our churches, it is evident that older adults are, and will continue to be, diverse and heterogeneous in their wants and needs. Leaders responsible for older-adult ministry in their congregations should do a careful analysis of the needs and wants of this group, just as for any other. In order to help leaders obtain additional materials useful for their ministry, this chapter provides a listing of resource information.

MINISTRIES WITH OLDER ADULTS WITHIN THE UNITED METHODIST CHURCH

Advocacy and Public Policy

The General Board of Church and Society
  100 Maryland Ave., NE
  Washington, DC 20002
  Phone: 800-967-0880 (toll free) or 202-488-5600
  Website: www.umc-gbcs.org

The General Board of Church and Society provides advocacy and public policy information on behalf of the needs of older adults.

Caring Couples Network
The General Board of Discipleship
Office of Family Ministries
PO Box 340003
Nashville, TN 37203-0003
Phone: 615-340-7170
Fax: 615-340-7071
Website: www.gbod.org/family

The Office of Family Ministries produces resources related to Caring Couples Network (CCN), which is a congregation-based system for marriage support. Churches enlist married couples with healthy marriages, many of whom are older couples, to serve as marriage advocates in the congregation and as mentor couples and families.

Center on Aging and Older-Adult Ministries
The General Board of Discipleship
PO Box 340003
Nashville, TN 37203-0003
Phone: 615-340-7173
Fax: 615-340-7071
Website: aging-umc.org

Established in 2000 by the General Board of Discipleship, the Center provides training and resource support for leaders of older adults in congregations and annual conferences. Printed resources, such as books, newsletters (*Center Sage*), and brochures, are made available. Training events and networking opportunities are conducted regularly.

Chaplaincy and Endorsement
The General Board of Higher Education and Ministry
PO Box 340007
Nashville, TN 37203-0007
Phone: 615-340-7411
Fax: 615-340-7358
E-mail: scrm@gbhem.org
Website: www.gbhem.org

The General Board of Higher Education and Ministry provides endorsement, support, and training for clergy serving as chaplains and in related ministries for the elderly in institutional settings.

Committee on Older-Adult Ministries
The General Board of Discipleship
Center on Aging and Older-Adult Ministries
PO Box 340003
Nashville, TN 37203-0003
Phone: 615-340-7173
Fax: 615-340-7071
Website: aging-umc.org

Established in 1992 by General Conference, the Committee on Older-Adult Ministries provides a forum for information sharing, cooperative planning, and joint program endeavors as determined in accordance with the responsibilities and objectives of the boards and agencies of The United Methodist Church. The Committee serves as an advocate for older-adult concerns and issues and supports ministries by, with, and for older adults.

Comprehensive Plan for Older-Adult Ministries
The General Board of Discipleship
Center on Aging and Older-Adult Ministries
PO Box 340003
Nashville, TN 37203-0003
Phone: 615-340-7173
Fax: 615-340-7071
Website: aging-umc.org

Established in 2000 by action of General Conference, the Comprehensive Plan provides for resources and grant funding to help annual conferences, districts, and local United Methodist congregations develop intentional, innovative, and creative ministries with older adults.

General Information
Curric-U-Phone
Phone: 800-251-8591 (toll free) or 615-749-6482

Provides answers to curriculum questions related to Cokesbury resources for Sunday school and other teaching and study materials.

InfoServ

Phone: 800-251-8140 (toll free)
Fax: 615-742-5423
E-mail: infoserv@umcom.org
Website: www.infoserv.umc.org

Provides information about the programs, resources, materials, benevolences, staff, or other matters related to The United Methodist Church.

Health and Welfare Ministries

Health and Welfare Ministries

General Board of Global Ministries
475 Riverside Dr., Room 330
New York, NY 10115
Phone: 212-870-3871
Fax: 212-870-3624
E-mail: hwmin@gbgm-umc.org
Website: gbgm-umc.org/health

Health and Welfare Ministries provides information concerning four basic models of congregation-based health ministries. The General Board of Global Ministries also provides information and support for ministry with people who are deaf and people who have disabilities.

United Methodist Association

601 W. Riverview Ave.
Dayton, OH 45406
Phone: 800-411-9901 (toll free) or 937-227-9494
Fax: 937-222-7364
E-mail: info@umassociation.org
Website: www.umassociation.org

The United Methodist Association is a national association of United Methodist-related ministries and individual professions concerned about the quality of healthcare in a faith-based setting. The mission of the Association is sharing, promoting, and strengthening the Wesleyan values of healing and caring, in cooperation with the connectional units of The United Methodist Church.

Mature Years Magazine
The United Methodist Publishing House
201 Eighth Ave., South
PO Box 801
Nashville, TN 37202
Phone: 800-672-1789 (toll free, Cokesbury)
Fax: 800-445-8189 (toll free, Cokesbury)
Website: www.cokesbury.com

Mature Years is a quarterly magazine containing leisure reading and Bible study based on the International Lessons/Uniform Series. Each large-print volume features articles and stories about mature adults, inspirational poetry, practical information about aging, insights into living and faith, and Bible lessons and daily meditations.

Men and Aging
General Commission on United Methodist Men
PO Box 340006
Nashville, TN 37203-0006
Phone: 615-340-7145
Fax: 615-340-1770
Website: www.gcumm.org

Information and resources are available for the organizing of local chapters of United Methodist men, for the development of programs for men, and for the faith formation of men.

Mission Volunteers
The General Board of Global Ministries
Mission Volunteers Office
475 Riverside Dr., Suite 330
New York, NY 10115
Phone: 800-554-8583 (toll free) or 212-870-3825
E-mail: voluntrs@gbgm-umc.org
Website: gbgm-umc.org/vim

Mission opportunities and programs planned by the General Board of Global Ministries include United Methodist Volunteers in Missions (UMVIM), Primetimers, and NOMADS. The purpose of Primetimers is to provide new service and learning experiences for older adults, offering opportunities for intentional education, faith-filled reflection, and cross-cultural appreciation in the context of Christian mission. The purpose of NOMADS is to offer people with recreational vehicles the opportunity to give their time and skills in special mission projects.

Publishing Resources

Cokesbury (The United Methodist Publishing House)
201 Eighth Ave., South
PO Box 801
Nashville, TN 37202
Phone: 800-672-1789 (toll free)
TDD/TT: 800-227-4091 (toll free)
Fax: 800-445-8189 (toll free)
Website: www.cokesbury.com

Discipleship Resources (The General Board of Discipleship)
PO Box 1616
Alpharetta, GA 30009-1616
Phone: 800-685-4370 (toll free)
Fax: 770-442-9742
Website: www.discipleshipresources.org

Service Center (The General Board of Global Ministries)
7820 Reading Rd., Caller No. 1800
Cincinnati, OH 45222-1800
Phone: 800-305-9857 (toll free) or 513-761-2100
Fax: 513-761-3722

Upper Room Books and Magazines (The General Board of Discipleship)
1908 Grand Ave.
PO Box 340004
Nashville, TN 37203-0004
Phone: 800-972-0433 (toll free)
Website: www.upperroom.org

Videos

EcuFilm

United Methodist Communications
PO Box 320
Nashville, TN 37202-0320
Phone: 800-251-4091 (toll free) or 615-242-6277
Website: www.ecufilm.com

EcuFilm, an ecumenical service, provides videos for sale and rental on topics related to aging issues and older-adult ministries.

Women and Aging

The General Board of Global Ministries — Women's Division
475 Riverside Dr., Room 1504
New York, NY 10115
Phone: 212-870-3752
Fax: 212-870-3736
Website: gbgm-umc.org/womens-division

The General Commission on the Status and Role of Women
1200 Davis St.
Evanston, IL 60201
Phone: 800-523-8390 (toll free) or 847-869-7330
Fax: 847-869-1466
E-mail: gcsrw@gcfa.org
Website: gcsrw.org

The General Commission on the Status and Role of Women provides advocacy and information on behalf of older women.

FORMAL EDUCATIONAL OPPORTUNITIES IN OLDER-ADULT MINISTRIES WITHIN THE UNITED METHODIST CHURCH

In addition to various training seminars and workshops on older-adult ministries conducted by boards and agencies, jurisdictions, annual conferences, districts, and local churches, there are various formal education opportunities through the church and church-related institutions that include certificates, certification, concentrations, specializations, and degrees.

Baldwin-Wallace College

275 Eastland Rd.
Berea, OH 44017
Phone: 440-826-2900
Website: www.bw.edu

Certificate program in gerontology

Boston University

53 Bay State Rd.
Boston, MA 02215
Phone: 617-353-5045
Website: www.bu.edu/gerontology

Louis Lowy Certificate in Gerontological Studies (Gerontology Center);
Doctor of Ministry degree in Pastoral Counseling with specialization in
gerontology

Duke University Divinity School

Box 90968
Durham NC 27708
Phone: 919-660-3400
Website: www.divinity.duke.edu

Course work and research through the Duke Institute on Care at the End
of Life, an interdisciplinary scholarship, teaching, and outreach institute

Garrett-Evangelical Theological Seminary

2121 Sheridan Rd.
Evanston, IL 60201
Phone: 847-866-3900
E-mail: seminary@northwestern.edu
Website: www.garrett.nwu.edu

Master of Arts degree in pastoral care and counseling with an emphasis in
older adults; Doctor of Ministry degree with a specialization in pastoral
care and an emphasis in older-adult ministries

The General Board of Higher Education and Ministry

PO Box 340007
Nashville, TN 37203-0007

Phone: 615-340-7375
Fax: 615-340-7377
E-mail: sddm@gbhem.org
Website: www.gbhem.org/certification/olderadults.html
Certification in older-adult ministry

Green Mountain College
One College Circle
Poultney, VT 05764
Phone: 800-776-6675 (toll free)
Website: www.greenmtn.edu
Gerontology as an area of study

McKendree College
701 College Rd.
Lebanon, IL 62254
Phone: 800-232-7228 (toll free) or 618-537-4481
Website: www.mckendree.edu
Gerontology as an area of study

Norman T. Allers Academy of Older-Adult Ministries
Southeast Jurisdiction Discipleship Ministries
PO Box 237
Lake Junaluska, NC 28745
Phone: 888-525-3586, ext. 2 (toll free)
E-mail: jmcswain@sejumc.org
Website: www.sejumc.org
Certification as a Fellow of the Academy of Older-Adult Ministries

Saint Paul School of Theology
5123 Truman Rd.
Kansas City, MO 64127
Phone: 816-483-9600
Website: www.spst.edu

Master of Divinity degree with specialization in gerontology;
Doctor of Ministry degree with specialization in gerontology

United Theological Seminary
1810 Harvard Blvd.
Dayton, OH 45406
Phone: 937-278-5817
E-mail: doctoralstudies@united.edu
Website: www.united.edu
Doctor of Ministry degree in ministry with the elderly

University of Evansville
1800 Lincoln Ave.
Evansville, IN 47722
Phone: 800-423-8633 (toll free)
Website: www.evansville.edu
Certificate program in gerontology

Wesley Theological Seminary
4500 Massachusetts Ave., NW
Washington, DC 20016
Phone: 800-882-4987 (toll free) or 202-885-6482
Fax: 202-885-8605
E-mail: swillhauck@wesleysem.edu
Website: www.wesleysem.edu
Certificate program in older-adult ministry

MINISTRY PROGRAM RESOURCES
Association for Couples in Marriage Enrichment (A.C.M.E.)
PO Box 10596
Winston-Salem, NC 27108
Phone: 800-634-8325 (toll free) or 336-724-1526
E-mail: acme@bettermarriages.org
Website: www.bettermarriages.org

A.C.M.E. is a network of people working for better marriages. A.C.M.E.'s aim is to offer opportunities for couples to build on their strengths and to equip them with skills and resources to develop a more satisfying relationship. Activities include weekend retreats, ongoing enrichment groups, skills-learning classes, workshops, seminars, and local chapter programs.

Body Recall

PO Box 412
Berea, KY 40403
Phone: 859-986-2181
Fax: 859-986-7580
Website: www.bodyrecallinc.org

Body Recall is an education program in physical exercise for lifetime fitness. Areas of focus include teacher training, visibility workshops, and resources to support a unique approach to teaching and coaching physical fitness with older adults.

Center for Aging, Religion, and Spirituality (CARS)

2481 Como Ave.
St. Paul, MN 55108
Phone: 651-641-3581
Fax: 651-641-3425
E-mail: cars@luthersem.edu
Website: www.luthersem.edu/cars

CARS provides educational opportunities and encourages research on religious and spiritual components for people engaged in various older-adult ministries. CARS also conducts specialized training through the Geriatric Pastoral Care Institute.

The Eden Alternative

Summer Hill Company, Inc.
The Eden Alternative
742 Turnpike Rd.
Sherburne, NY 13460
Phone: 607-674-5232
Fax: 607-674-6723
E-mail: contact@edenalt.com
Website: www.edenalt.com

The Eden Alternative (EA) is a tool for improving the quality of life for older adults in nursing homes and other long-term healthcare settings. EA is committed to creating better social and physical environments for people in nursing homes in an effort to eliminate the plagues of loneliness, helplessness, and boredom.

Fanlight Productions

4196 Washington St.
Boston, MA 02131
Phone: 800-937-4113 (toll free)
E-mail: info@fanlight.com
Website: www.fanlight.com

Fanlight is a distributor of videos for leaders of older-adult ministries on topics such as aging, caregiving, death and dying, elder abuse, end-of-life care, grief and recovery, hospice and palliative care, long-term care, and sexuality and aging.

Health Ministries Association (HMA)

980 Canton St.
Building 1, Suite B
Roswell, GA 30075
Phone: 800-280-9919 (toll free) or 770-640-9955
Fax: 770-640-1095
E-mail: hma@hmassoc.org
Website: www.healthministriesassociation.org

HMA is an interfaith membership organization that seeks to encourage, support, and develop whole-person ministries leading to the integration of faith and health. In addition to resources, education, and advocacy, HMA brings together people of faith who work to improve the health of people and the communities they live in.

Lifetapes Communications, Inc.

Phone: 888-777-5585 (toll free)
E-mail: lifetapes@agingparents.com
Website: www.agingparents.com

Lifetapes Communications provides resources titled *Aging Parents* for families caring for aging parents. Resources include videos, workbooks, facilitator manuals, and more. The various *Aging Parents* products include *Aging Parents: The Family Survival Guide, Aging Parents: The Seminar, Aging Parents: The Training and Marketing Guide,* and *Aging Parents: Planning for the Future.*

Marriage Encounter–United Methodist

Phone: 866-633-3862 (toll free)
Website: www.encounter.org

Marriage Encounter is a marriage-enhancement program designed for married couples. It helps individuals examine where they are in their relationship with each other, think about where they want to be, and plan how to get there. Marriage Encounter is structured around weekend retreats.

Marriage Enrichment Workshops

Phone: 800-726-7424 (toll free)
Website: www.marriageenrichment.org

Marriage Enrichment Workshops are designed for couples who want to enhance their communication skills. The workshops, which are held in cooperation with local churches, are conducted as weekend retreats, midweek sessions, and in-church/in-home weekends.

Park Ridge Center

211 E. Ontario, Suite 800
Chicago, IL 60611-3215
Phone: 847-384-3502 (toll free)
Fax: 312-266-6086

The Park Ridge Center for the Study of Health, Faith, and Ethics produces the educational program "Retrieving Spiritual Traditions in Long-Term Care for the Elderly." This comprehensive program enables participants to confront cultural stereotypes of aging and the elderly, provides an understanding of the Christian view of aging, and increases awareness of the possibility of spiritual growth in the elderly.

Shepherd's Centers of America

One W. Armour Blvd., Suite 201
Kansas City, MO 64111
Phone: 800-547-7073 (toll free) or 816-960-2022
Fax: 816-960-1083
E-mail: staff@shepherdcenters.org
Website: www.shepherdcenters.org

Shepherd's Centers of America is an interfaith umbrella organization of nearly 100 independent Shepherd's Centers throughout the United States.

Each center provides a program that is a ministry by and with older adults, rather than a ministry to them. The various programs, activities, and home services of Shepherd's Centers are built around four main emphases: life maintenance, life enrichment, life reorganization, and celebration.

Spiritual Eldering Institute
970 Aurora Ave.
Boulder, CO 80302
Phone: 303-449-7243
Fax: 303-938-1277
E-mail: info@spiritualeldering.org
Website: www.spiritualeldering.org

The Spiritual Eldering Institute (SEI) is a multi-faith organization dedicated to the spiritual dimensions of aging and conscious living, to affirming the importance of the elder years, and to teaching individuals how to harvest life's wisdom and transform it into a legacy for future generations. SEI works with communities and organizations to develop Sage-ing Programs and Centers and provides training for leaders to share in this work.

Stephen Ministries
2045 Innerbelt Business Center Dr.
St. Louis, MO 63114
Phone: 314-428-2600
Fax: 314-428-7888
Website: www.stephenministries.org

Stephen Ministries is a program of training, resources, and support for Christian caring to people in need. With Stephen Ministries, people no longer have to go through crises and difficulties alone. Stephen Ministers walk alongside people in need for as long as necessary, providing the emotional support and spiritual care they need. Stephen Ministers are lay Christians selected, trained, and supervised by their congregation's Stephen Leaders to provide effective, one-to-one Christian care to others.

Terra Nova Films
9848 S. Winchester Ave.
Chicago, IL 60643
Phone: 800-779-8491 (toll free)

Fax: 773-881-3368
E-mail: tnf@terranova.org
Website: www.terranova.org

Terra Nova produces and distributes a large selection of films on aging and elderhood. Some of the many topics include spirituality, intimacy, inter-generational relationships, positive images of aging, mental health, elder abuse, disabilities, healthcare, Alzheimer's disease, family caregiving, women and aging, and aging in diverse cultures.

Willowgreen Productions, Publishing, and Consulting
10351 Dawson's Creek Blvd., Suite B
Fort Wayne, IN 46802
Phone: 260-490-2222
Fax: 260-497-9622
E-mail: jmiller@willowgreen.com
Website: www.willowgreen.com

Willowgreen is committed to providing education, encouragement, support, and hope in the form of original printed, photographic, audiovisual, and multimedia resources as well as live presentations and keynote addresses. The purpose is to help all people, including older adults, experience inspiration and spirituality, encounter hope in the face of loss and grief, and provide support for managing transitions and caregiving.

NATIONAL & INTERNATIONAL ORGANIZATIONS

Administration on Aging (AoA)
One Massachusetts Ave.
Washington, DC 20201
Phone: 202-619-0724
          800-677-1116 (toll free, Eldercare Locator)
E-mail: aoainfo@aoa.gov
Website: www.aoa.gov

The Administration on Aging is the federal agency dedicated to policy development and to the planning and delivery of supportive home- and community-based services to older adults and their caregivers. The AoA works through a federal, state, tribal, and local partnership called the National Network on Aging.

Alzheimer's Association

225 North Michigan Ave., Suite 1700
Chicago, IL 60601
Phone: 800-272-3900 (toll free) or 312-335-8700
TTY: 312-335-8882
Fax: 312-335-1110
E-mail: info@alz.org
Website: www.alz.org

The Alzheimer's Association is a nonprofit organization offering information and support services to people with Alzheimer's disease and their families. Contact the 24-hour, toll-free number to link with local chapters and community resources. The Association funds research to find a cure and provides information on caregiving. A free catalog of educational publications is available in English and in Spanish.

Alzheimer's Disease Education and Referral (ADEAR) Center

PO Box 8250
Silver Spring, MD 20907-8250
Phone: 800-438-4380 (toll free) or 301-495-3311
Fax: 301-495-3334
E-mail: adear@alzheimers.org
Website: www.alzheimers.org

The ADEAR Center, funded by the National Institute on Aging, distributes information about Alzheimer's disease to health professionals, patients and their families, and the public.

American Association for Marriage and Family Therapy (AAMFT)

112 South Alfred St.
Alexandria, VA 22314
Phone: 703-838-9808
Fax: 703-838-9805
E-mail: memberservice@aamft.org
Website: www.aamft.org

AAMFT is a professional association that provides referrals to marriage and family therapists and offers publications on topics such as divorce, depression, and sexual problems.

American Association of Homes and Services for the Aging (AAHSA)

2519 Connecticut Ave., NW
Washington, DC 20008-1520
Phone: 202-783-2242
Fax: 202-783-2255
E-mail: info@aahsa.org
Website: www.aahsa.org

AAHSA is a nonprofit organization providing older adults with services and information on housing, healthcare, and community involvement.

American Association of Retired Persons (AARP)

601 E St., NW
Washington, DC 20049
Phone: 800-424-3410 (toll free) or 202-434-2277
Website: www.aarp.org

AARP is a nonprofit organization that advocates for older adults' health, rights, and life choices. Local chapters provide information and services on crime prevention, consumer protection, and income tax preparation. Members can join group health, auto, life, and home insurance programs; investment plans; or a discount mail-order pharmacy service. Publications are available on housing, health, exercise, retirement planning, money management, leisure, and travel.

American Cancer Society (ACS)

1599 Clifton Rd., NE
Atlanta, GA 30329
Phone: 800-227-2345 (toll free)
Website: www.cancer.org

The American Cancer Society is a national, community-based volunteer health organization providing information on cancer and its prevention. The Society sponsors a variety of educational programs. Local ACS offices sponsor services for cancer patients and their families, including self-help groups, transportation programs, and limited financial aid. Resources are available in English and in Spanish.

American Diabetes Association (ADA)

1701 North Beauregard St.
Alexandria, VA 22311
Phone: 800-342-2383 (toll free) or 703-549-1500
Website: www.diabetes.org

ADA provides information and educational materials on preventing, treating, and living with diabetes. The Association has specific outreach programs for racial and minority communities. Local ADA chapters offer support and referrals to community agencies and services.

American Heart Association (AHA)

7272 Greenville Ave.
Dallas, TX 75231
Phone: 800-242-8721 (toll free)
Website: www.americanheart.org

AHA is a nonprofit organization funding research and providing information on the diagnosis, treatment, and prevention of heart diseases and stroke. Cookbooks and guides to heart attack treatment and fitness are available.

American Lung Association (ALA)

61 Broadway, 6th Floor
New York, NY 10006
Phone: 800-586-4872 (toll free) or 212-315-8700
Website: www.lungusa.org

ALA is dedicated to the prevention, cure, and control of lung diseases, such as asthma, emphysema, tuberculosis, and lung cancer. The Association offers community service programs, public health education, advocacy, and research.

American Parkinson Disease Association (APDA)

1250 Hylan Blvd., Suite 4B
Staten Island, NY 10305
Phone: 800-223-2732 (toll free)
          888-400-2732 (toll free, local information and referral center)
Fax: 718-981-4399
E-mail: apda@apdaparkinson.org
Website: www.apdaparkinson.org

APDA funds research to find a cure for Parkinson's disease. APDA's toll-free line refers callers to local chapters for information on community services, specialists, and treatments. Publications and educational materials are available on Parkinson's disease, speech therapy, exercise, diet, and aids for daily living.

American Society on Aging (ASA)
833 Market St., Suite 511
San Francisco, CA 94103
Phone: 800-537-9728 (toll free) or 415-974-9600
Fax: 415-974-0300
E-mail: info@asaging.org
Website: www.asaging.org

ASA is a nonprofit organization providing information about medical and social practice, research, and policy pertinent to the health of older adults. Educational programs and seminars are planned on a regular basis. Membership and subscriptions to *Generations,* a quarterly journal, and *Aging Today,* the Society's bimonthly news magazine, are available. Of particular interest to church leaders is the section Forum on Religion: Spirituality and Aging (FORSA), which publishes its own newsletter.

American Stroke Association (ASA)
7272 Greenville Ave.
Dallas, TX 75231
Phone: 888-478-7653 (toll free)
Fax: 214-706-5231
E-mail: strokeassociation@heart.org
Website: www.strokeassociation.org

A division of the American Heart Association, ASA provides the Warmline, a toll-free information and referral service offering free stroke support information to stroke survivors, caregivers, family members, and healthcare professionals. Callers receive support and can request free information. ASA publishes *Stroke Connection,* a magazine for survivors and their families.

Arthritis Foundation (AF)
PO Box 7669
Atlanta, GA 30357
Phone: 800-283-7800 (toll free) or 404-965-7888

Fax: 404-872-9559
E-mail: help@arthritis.org
Website: www.arthritis.org

AF is a nonprofit organization focusing on research and information to cure, prevent, or better treat arthritis and related diseases. Contact AF for information on arthritis, related diseases, and referrals to local chapters, specialists, or support groups. Publications and videos are available on topics such as self-help and exercise therapy.

Better Hearing Institute (BHI)

515 King St., Suite 420
Alexandria, VA 22314
Phone: 888-432-7435 (toll free) or 800-327-9355 (toll free, Helpline)
E-mail: mail@betterhearing.org
Website: www.betterhearing.org

BHI is a nonprofit organization providing information on hearing aids and on medical, surgical, and rehabilitation options for improving hearing loss. Contact the BHI Helpline for facts on hearing loss and a list of publications.

Better Vision Institute (BVI)

1700 Diagonal Rd., Suite 500
Alexandria, VA 22314
Phone: 877-642-3253
Website: www.visionsite.org

BVI provides news and information on vision health and care. Contact the Institute for facts on the detection, treatment, and prevention of eye diseases. Publications include fact sheets on cataracts, nutrition, care of eyeglasses, diabetes, and vision care.

Children of Aging Parents (CAPS)

1609 Woodbourne Rd., Suite 302A
Levittown, PA 19057
Phone: 800-227-7294 (toll free) or 215-945-6900
Website: www.caps4caregivers.org

CAPS is a nonprofit organization that provides support services to caregivers of older people. It serves as a clearinghouse for information on elder care resources and issues, including "Instant Aging" workshops to help caregivers understand the needs of older adults.

Eldercare Locator

Phone: 800-677-1116 (toll free)
E-mail: eldercare_locator@aoa.gov
Website: www.eldercare.gov

The Eldercare Locator is a nationwide, directory-assistance service help-ing older people and their caregivers locate local support and resources for older Americans. It is funded by the Administration on Aging.

Elderhostel

11 Avenue de Lafayette
Boston, MA 02111-1746
Phone: 877-426-8056 (toll free)
      978-323-4141 (outside the U.S. or Canada)
TTY: 877-426-2167 (toll free)
Fax: 617-426-0701
E-mail: registration@elderhostel.org
Website: www.elderhostel.org

Elderhostel is a nonprofit organization providing educational travel pro-grams to people 55 years or older. Their catalogs list thousands of national and international programs.

Elderweb

1305 Chadwick Dr.
Normal, IL 61761
Phone: 309-451-3319
Fax: 866-422-8995
E-mail: info@elderweb.com
Website: www.elderweb.com

Elderweb is a research website for older people, professionals, and fami-lies seeking information on elder care and long-term care. Visit Elderweb for links to other websites and for news and information on legal, finan-cial, medical, and housing issues for older adults.

Generations United (GU)

122 C St., NW, Suite 820
Washington, DC 20001
Phone: 202-638-1263

Fax: 202-638-7555
E-mail: gu@gu.org
Website: www.gu.org

GU focuses solely on promoting intergenerational strategies, programs, and policies. GU provides a forum for those working with children, youth, and older adults to explore areas of common ground while celebrating the richness of each generation.

Gerontological Society of America (GSA)
1030 15th St., NW, Suite 250
Washington, DC 20005
Phone: 202-842-1275
Fax: 202-842-1150
E-mail: geron@geron.org
Website: www.geron.org

GSA is a professional organization providing information, advocacy, and support for research into the study of aging. GSA has a database of information on biological and social aspects of aging, links to aging information resources, and referrals to researchers and specialists in gerontology. GSA distributes publications on a variety of aging-related topics.

Global Action on Aging (GAoA)
PO Box 20022
New York, NY 10025
Phone: 212-557-3163
Fax: 212-557-3164
E-mail: globalaging@globalaging.org
Website: www.globalaging.org

Global Action on Aging is an international, grass-roots citizen group that works on issues of concern to older people. It reports on older people's needs and potential within the globalized world economy and advocates by, with, and for older people worldwide.

Gray Panthers (GP)
733 15th St., NW, Suite 437
Washington, DC 20005
Phone: 800-280-5362 (toll free) or 202-737-6637
Fax: 202-737-1160

E-mail: info@graypanthers.org

Website: www.graypanthers.org

Gray Panthers is a national advocacy organization of activists concentrating on social and economic issues. Local chapters organize intergenerational groups to address issues, such as universal healthcare, Medicare, preservation of Social Security, affordable housing, and discrimination.

Meals on Wheels Association of America (MOWAA)

1414 Prince St., Suite 302

Alexandria, VA 22314

Phone: 703-548-5558

Website: www.mowaa.org

MOWAA is a national, nonprofit organization providing training and grants to programs that provide food to people who are frail, disabled, at-risk, or homebound.

National Adult Day Services Association (NADSA)

8201 Greensboro Dr., Suite 300

McLean, VA 22102

Phone: 866-890-7357 (toll free) or 703-610-9035

Fax: 703-610-9005

E-mail: info@nadsa.org

Website: www.nadsa.org

NADSA is committed to providing the growing adult day services industry with effective national advocacy, educational and networking opportunities, technical assistance, research, and communication services.

National Asian Pacific Center on Aging (NAPCA)

PO Box 21668

Seattle, WA 98101

Phone: 206-624-1221

Fax: 206-624-1023

E-mail: web@napca.org

Website: www.napca.org

NAPCA is a nonprofit agency dedicated to serving aging Asians and Pacific Islanders. It offers employment programs, multilingual community forums, and healthcare education. The Center works with elders, policy makers, program administrators, and community leaders. Publications include translated healthcare materials.

National Association for Hispanic Elderly

234 East Colorado Blvd., Suite 300
Pasadena, CA 91101
Phone: 626-564-1988
Fax: 626-564-2659

The National Association for Hispanic Elderly is a national, private, non-profit organization providing a variety of services for older Hispanic people. Resources include a national Hispanic research center, research and consultation for organizations seeking to reach older Spanish-speaking people, and dissemination of written and audiovisual materials in English and in Spanish.

National Caucus and Center on Black Aged, Inc. (NCBA)

1220 L St., NW, Suite 800
Washington, DC 20005
Phone: 202-637-8400
E-mail: info@ncba-aged.org
Website: www.ncba-aged.org

NCBA is a national organization providing health and social service information, advocacy, and assistance to African Americans and low-income older adults. Contact NCBA for information on its local chapters and programs, including senior employment and training, housing, health promotion, and advocacy.

National Center on Elder Abuse (NCEA)

1201 15th St., NW, Suite 350
Washington, DC 20005
Phone: 202-898-2586
Fax: 202-898-2583
E-mail: ncea@nasua.org
Website: www.elderabusecenter.org

NCEA serves as a clearinghouse for information on abuse and neglect of the elderly and can provide referrals to agencies and specialists. Publications are available on prevention of abuse and neglect and on state regulations.

National Center on Women and Aging

The Heller School for Social Policy and Management
MS 035
Brandeis University
Waltham, MA 02454-9110
Phone: 800-929-1995 (toll free) or 781-736-3866
Fax: 781-736-3865
E-mail: natwomctr@brandeis.edu
Website: www.brandeis.edu/heller/national

The National Center on Women and Aging focuses on older women's issues and provides information and publications on women's health, caregiving, income security, and housing as well as prevention of crime and violence toward older women.

National Council on the Aging (NCOA)

300 D St., SW, Suite 801
Washington, DC 20024
Phone: 800-424-9046 (toll free) or 202-479-1200
Fax: 202-479-0735
E-mail: info@ncoa.org
Website: www.ncoa.org

NCOA is a private, nonprofit organization providing information, training, technical assistance, advocacy, and leadership in all aspects of aging services and issues. NCOA publications are available on topics such as lifelong learning, senior center services, adult daycare, long-term care, financial issues, senior housing, intergenerational programs, and volunteers in aging.

National Family Caregivers Association (NFCA)

10400 Connecticut Ave., #500
Kensington, MD 20895-3944
Phone: 800-896-3650 (toll free)
Fax: 301-942-2302
E-mail: info@nfcacares.org
Website: www.nfcacares.org

NFCA is a grass roots organization providing advocacy, support, and information for family members who care for chronically ill, older, or disabled relatives. There is no charge for family members to be on the mailing list and to receive the newsletter, *Take Care!*

National Hispanic Council on Aging (NHCoA)

2713 Ontario Rd., NW
Washington, DC 20009
Phone: 202-265-1288
Fax: 202-745-2522
E-mail: nhcoa@nhcoa.org
Website: www.nhcoa.org

NHCoA is a national organization providing advocacy, education, and information for older Hispanic adults. Contact the Council for facts and resources on health, employment, housing, strengthening families, and building communities as well as referrals to local Council chapters. Publications are available in English and in Spanish.

National Hospice and Palliative Care Organization (NHPCO)

1700 Diagonal Rd., Suite 625
Alexandria, VA 22314
Phone: 800-646-6460 (toll free) or 703-837-1500
E-mail: info@nhpco.org
Website: www.nhpco.org

NHPCO is a nonprofit membership organization working to enhance the quality of life for individuals who are terminally ill and advocating for people in the final stage of life. Contact NHPCO for information, resources, and referrals to local hospice services. Publications, fact sheets, and website resources are available on topics such as how to find and evaluate hospice services.

National Indian Council on Aging (NICOA)

10501 Montgomery Blvd., NE, Suite 210
Albuquerque, NM 87111
Phone: 505-292-2001
E-mail: dave@nicoa.org
Website: www.nicoa.org

NICOA provides services, advocacy, and information on aging issues for older American Indian and Alaska Native people. Contact NICOA for information about its resources and support groups serving the national Indian community, including the newsletter *Elder Visions*.

National Institute on Aging (NIA)
Building 31, Room 5C27
31 Center Dr., MSC 2292
Bethesda, MD 20892
Phone: 800-222-2225 (toll free) or 301-496-1752
TTY: 800-222-4225 (toll free)
Website: www.nih.gov/nia

NIA, part of the National Institutes of Health, conducts and supports biomedical, social, and behavioral research on aging processes, diseases, and the special problems and needs of older adults. NIA develops and disseminates publications on topics such as the biology of aging, exercise, doctor/patient communication, and menopause. The Institute produces *Age Pages,* a series of fact sheets for consumers on a wide range of subjects, including nutrition, medications, forgetfulness, sleep, driving, and long-term care.

National Interfaith Coalition on Aging (NICA)
National Council on the Aging (NCOA)
300 D St., SW, Suite 801
Washington, DC 20024
Phone: 800-424-9046 (toll free) or 202-479-1200
Fax: 202-479-0735
Website: www.ncoa.org

NICA, a constituent unit of NCOA, consists of individuals and organizations of various faith traditions concerned with issues of religion, spirituality, and aging. NICA provides networking opportunities, training events, and educational programs.

National Long-Term Care Ombudsman Resource Center (NLTCORC)
1424 16th St., NW, Suite 202
Washington, DC 20036
Phone: 202-332-2275
Fax: 202-332-2949
E-mail: ombudcenter@nccnhr.org
Website: www.ltcombudsman.org

NLTCORC, which is operated by the National Citizens' Coalition for Nursing Home Reform, supports groups under federal mandate to identify and resolve residents' problems at long-term care facilities. Contact the Center for information and publications on nursing home reform, adult care, and state long-term care ombudsman programs.

National Osteoporosis Foundation (NOF)

1232 22nd St., NW
Washington, DC 20037-1292
Phone: 202-223-2226
Fax: 202-223-2237
Website: www.nof.org

NOF is a nonprofit, voluntary health organization dedicated to promoting lifelong bone health to reduce the widespread prevalence of osteoporosis and related fractures. The Foundation provides general information on osteoporosis for free, and its quarterly newsletter and booklets are available through membership.

National Resource Center on Native American Aging (NRCNAA)

Center for Rural Health
PO Box 9037
Grand Forks, ND 58202-9037
Phone: 800-896-7628 (toll free) or 701-777-3437
Fax: 701-777-6779
Website: www.und.edu/dept/nrcnaa

The Resource Center, funded by the Administration on Aging, provides support, advocacy, and information for older Native Americans, including American Indians, Alaska Natives, and Native Hawaiians. Contact the Center for legal information and references, geriatric leadership training, cultural awareness, and a variety of publications.

National Senior Games Association (NSGA)

PO Box 82059
Baton Rouge, LA 70884-2059
Phone: 225-766-6800
Website: www.nsga.com

NSGA is a nonprofit organization promoting healthy lifestyles for older adults through education, fitness, and sports. Its website announces Association events and activities.

Older Women's League (OWL)

1750 New York Ave., NW, Suite 350
Washington, DC 20006
Phone: 800-825-3695 (toll free) or 202-783-6686
      800-863-1539 (toll free, PowerLine)
Fax: 202-628-0458
E-mail: owlinfo@owl-national.org
Website: www.owl-national.org

OWL is a national organization advocating for the special concerns of older women. Contact OWL's 24-hour PowerLine for information about legal and political activity related to healthcare, access to housing, economic security, individual rights, and violence against women and older people. OWL newsletters are available.

Senior Job Bank

PO Box 30064
Savannah, GA 31410
E-mail: info@seniorjobbank.org
Website: www.seniorjobbank.org

Senior Job Bank is an online resource that provides free job information and resources for members. Contact the Job Bank to find listings for occasional, part-time, flexible, temporary, or full-time jobs for older people.

SeniorNet (SN)

121 Second St., 7th Floor
San Francisco, CA 94105
Phone: 800-747-6848 (toll free) or 415-495-4990
Fax: 415-495-3999
Website: www.seniornet.org

SeniorNet is a nonprofit, educational organization that provides information and services to help older people become computer literate. Locally funded SN teaching sites offer introductory computer classes on various topics and provide older people with discounts on computer hardware, software, and publications. Members can access SN from any online computer and order publications on buying and using computers.

Social Security Administration (SSA)

Office of Public Inquiries
Windsor Park Building
6401 Security Blvd.
Baltimore, MD 21235
Phone: 800-772-1213 (toll free)
TTY: 800-325-0778 (toll free)
Fax: 410-965-0695
Website: www.ssa.gov

SSA, part of the federal government, is the agency responsible for Social Security retirement programs, survivor benefits, disability insurance, and Supplemental Security Income.

SPRY Foundation

10 G St., NE, Suite 600
Washington, DC 20002
Phone: 202-216-0401
Fax: 202-216-0779
E-mail: info@spry.org
Website: www.spry.org

SPRY (Setting Priorities for Retirement Years) is a nonprofit foundation that develops research and education programs to help older adults plan for a healthy and financially secure future.

United Seniors Health Council (USHC)

300 D St., SW, Suite 801
Washington, DC 20024
Phone: 202-479-6678
Fax: 202-479-6660
Website: www.ncoa.org

USHC is a nonprofit organization dedicated to helping older consumers, caregivers, and professionals. The Council produces publications on topics such as financial planning, managed care, and long-term care insurance. It also produces *Eldergames,* a comprehensive series of materials designed to stimulate the imagination and memories of older adults.

Well Spouse Foundation (WSF)

63 West Main St., Suite H
Freehold, NJ 07728
Phone: 800-838-0879 (toll free) or 732-577-8899
Fax: 732-577-8644
E-mail: info@wellspouse.org
Website: www.wellspouse.org

Well Spouse is a nonprofit association of spousal caregivers that offers support to the wives, husbands, and partners of chronically ill or disabled people. The Foundation has lists of support groups nationwide and sponsors recreational respite opportunities.

SCRIPTURES ON AGING AND OLDER ADULTS

(Texts are from the New Revised Standard Version, unless otherwise noted.)

Old Testament (Hebrew Scriptures)

Genesis 5:27. Thus all the days of Methuselah were nine hundred sixty-nine years; and he died.

Genesis 6:3. Then the LORD said, "My spirit shall not abide in mortals forever, for they are flesh; their days shall be one hundred twenty years."

Genesis 12:4. So Abram went, as the LORD had told him; and Lot went with him. Abram was seventy-five years old when he departed from Haran.

Genesis 17:17. Then Abraham fell on his face and laughed, and said to himself, "Can a child be born to a man who is a hundred years old? Can Sarah, who is ninety years old, bear a child?"

Genesis 18:11-12. Now Abraham and Sarah were old, advanced in age; it had ceased to be with Sarah after the manner of women. So Sarah laughed to herself, saying, "After I have grown old, and my husband is old, shall I have pleasure?"

Genesis 21:5. Abraham was a hundred years old when his son Isaac was born to him.

Exodus 7:7. Moses was eighty years old and Aaron eighty-three when they spoke to Pharaoh.

Exodus 20:12. Honor your father and your mother, so that your days may be long in the land that the LORD your God is giving you.

Leviticus 19:32. You shall rise before the aged, and defer to the old; and you shall fear your God.

Numbers 8:24-25. This applies to the Levites: from twenty-five years old and upward they shall begin to do duty in the service of the tent of meeting; and from the age of fifty years they shall retire from the duty of the service and serve no more.

Deuteronomy 32:7. Remember the days of old, consider the years long past; ask your father, and he will inform you; your elders, and they will tell you.

Ruth 1:12a. Turn back, my daughters, go your way, for I am too old to have a husband.

1 Samuel 2:22a; 3:1a. Now Eli was very old.... The boy Samuel was ministering to the LORD under Eli.

Job 5:26. You shall come to your grave in ripe old age, as a shock of grain comes up to the threshing floor in its season.

Job 12:12. Is wisdom with the aged, and understanding in length of days? (NRSV). Wisdom is with the aged; and understanding in length of days (RSV).

Psalm 31:10. For my life is spent with sorrow, and my years with sighing; my strength fails because of my misery, and my bones waste away.

Psalm 37:25. I have been young, and now am old, yet I have not seen the righteous forsaken or their children begging bread.

Psalm 71:9. Do not cast me off in the time of old age; do not forsake me when my strength is spent.

Psalm 71:18. So even to old age and gray hairs, O God, do not forsake me, until I proclaim your might to all the generations to come.

Psalm 90:10. The days of our life are seventy years, or perhaps eighty, if we are strong; even then their span is only toil and trouble; they are soon gone, and we fly away.

Psalm 92:12, 14. The righteous flourish like the palm tree, and grow like a cedar in Lebanon.… In old age they still produce fruit; they are always green and full of sap.

Psalm 148:12-13. Young men and women alike, old and young together! Let them praise the name of the Lord, for his name alone is exalted; his glory is above earth and heaven.

Proverbs 1:8. Hear, my child, your father's instruction, and do not reject your mother's teaching.

Proverbs 16:31. Gray hair is a crown of glory; it is gained in a righteous life.

Proverbs 20:20. If you curse father or mother, your lamp will go out in utter darkness.

Proverbs 20:29. The glory of youths is their strength, but the beauty of the aged is their gray hair.

Proverbs 23:22. Listen to your father who begot you, and do not despise your mother when she is old.

Proverbs 30:17. The eye that mocks a father and scorns to obey a mother will be pecked out by the ravens of the valley and eaten by the vultures.

Ecclesiastes 4:13. Better is a poor but wise youth than an old but foolish king, who will no longer take advice.

Isaiah 46:3a, 4. Listen to me, O house of Jacob,…even to your old age I am he, even when you turn gray I will carry you. I have made, and I will bear; I will carry and will save.

Joel 2:28. Then afterward I will pour out my spirit on all flesh; your sons and your daughters shall prophesy, your old men shall dream dreams, and your young men shall see visions.

Zechariah 8:4. Thus says the Lord of hosts: Old men and old women shall again sit in the streets of Jerusalem, each with staff in hand because of their great age.

New Testament

Luke 2:36-37. There was also a prophet, Anna… She was of a great age, having lived with her husband seven years after her marriage, then as a widow to the age of eighty-four. She never left the temple but worshiped there with fasting and prayer night and day.

Luke 5:39. And no one after drinking old wine desires new wine, but says, "The old is good."

John 3:4. Nicodemus said to him, "How can anyone be born after having grown old? Can one enter a second time into the mother's womb and be born?"

John 21:18. Very truly, I tell you, when you were younger, you used to fasten your own belt and to go wherever you wished. But when you grow old, you will stretch out your hands, and someone else will fasten a belt around you and take you where you do not wish to go.

Acts 2:17. In the last days it will be, God declares, that I will pour out my Spirit upon all flesh, and your sons and your daughters shall prophesy, and your young men shall see visions, and your old men shall dream dreams.

2 Corinthians 4:16. For this reason we never become discouraged. Even though our physical being is gradually decaying, yet our spiritual being is renewed day after day (TEV).

Ephesians 6:2-3. "Honor your father and mother"—this is the first commandment with a promise: "so that it may be well with you and you may live long on the earth."

1 Timothy 5:1-2. Do not speak harshly to an older man, but speak to him as to a father,…to older women as mothers.

1 Timothy 5:3. Honor widows who are really widows.

2 Timothy 4:7. I have fought the good fight, I have finished the race, I have kept the faith.

Titus 2:2-3. Tell the older men to be temperate, serious, prudent, and sound in faith, in love, and in endurance. Likewise, tell the older women to be reverent in behavior, not to be slanderers or slaves to drink; they are to teach what is good.

Hebrews 5:12b-14. You need milk, not solid food; for everyone who lives on milk, being still an infant, is unskilled in the word of righteousness. But solid food is for the mature, for those whose faculties have been trained by practice to distinguish good from evil.

James 1:27. Religion that is pure and undefiled before God, the Father, is this: to care for orphans and widows in their distress, and to keep oneself unstained by the world.

1 Peter 5:5. You who are younger must accept the authority of the elders.

PRINTED RESOURCES

Resources published by Discipleship Resources may be ordered online at www.discipleshipresources.org; by phone at 800-972-0433; by fax at 615-340-7590; or by mail from Customer Services, PO Box 340012, Nashville, TN 37203-0012.

Aging: Concepts and Controversies (Fourth Edition), by Harry R. Moody (Thousand Oaks: Pine Forge Press, 2000). An excellent resource that helps readers reflect on many of the issues impacting both aging people and our aging society.

Aging: God's Challenge to Church and Synagogue, by Richard H. Gentzler, Jr. and Donald F. Clingan (Nashville: Discipleship Resources, 1996). This valuable resource provides practical ideas and important information necessary for understanding our aging society and "graying" congregations.

Aging, Spirituality, and Religion: A Handbook, edited by Melvin A. Kimble, Susan H. McFadden, James W. Ellor, and James J. Seeber (Minneapolis: Fortress Press, 1995). This book examines the ways religion and spirituality are experienced by aging people within an aging society.

Aging, Spirituality, and Religion: A Handbook (Volume 2), edited by Melvin A. Kimble and Susan H. McFadden (Minneapolis: Fortress Press, 2003). This resource offers examples of how religion and spirituality are encountered in the growth experiences and life crises of older adults.

Aging Well: Surprising Guideposts to a Happier Life From the Landmark Harvard Study of Adult Development, by George E. Vaillant, M.D. (New York: Little, Brown and Co., 2002). This book is based on what is arguably the longest study of aging in the world: the Study of Adult Development at Harvard University.

And Not One Bird Stopped Singing: Coping With Transition and Loss in Aging, by Doris Moreland Jones (Nashville: Upper Room Books, 1997). This book helps the reader look openly at his or her bereavement and grief. A valuable resource for people facing loss of any kind.

Building a Ministry for Homebound and Nursing-Home Residents, by Marie White Webb (Nashville: Discipleship Resources, 2003). A practical guide for people who already are, and those who want to be, engaged in ministry with people who are homebound and nursing-home residents.

Deciding About Life's End: A United Methodist Resource Book About Advance Directives. Available from the Service Center of the General Board of Global Ministries, 7820 Reading Rd., Caller 1800, Cincinnati, OH 45222-1800; 800-305-9857 (toll free) or 513-761-2100.

A Deepening Love Affair: The Gift of God in Later Life, by Jane Marie Thibault (Nashville: Upper Room Books, 1993). A classic book on spirituality in life's later years, with ways to become aware of your gifts.

Designing an Older-Adult Ministry, by Richard H. Gentzler, Jr. (Nashville: Discipleship Resources, 1999). A valuable how-to resource that provides information about organizing and sustaining an intentional ministry by, with, and for older adults in local church settings.

Engaging in Ministry With Older Adults, by Dosia Carlson (Bethesda, MD: Alban Institute, 1997). A helpful and practical book describing various models for older-adult ministry.

Fire in the Soul: A Prayer Book for the Later Years, by Richard Lyon Morgan (Nashville: Upper Room Books, 2000). A large-print guide that helps older adults seek God's help in meeting late-life challenges.

Forty-Sixty: A Study for Midlife Adults Who Want to Make a Difference, by Richard H. Gentzler, Jr. and Craig Kennet Miller (Nashville: Discipleship Resources, 2001). A small-group study book for Baby Boomers and midlife adults who are personally confronting the many issues of aging.

Guidelines for Leading Your Congregation: 2001–2004—Adult Ministries, by Richard H. Gentzler, Jr. and William Crenshaw (Nashville: Cokesbury, 2000). A how-to guide that provides practical ideas and models for adult ministry (including older-adult ministry) in congregational settings.

How to Care for Aging Parents, by Virginia Morris (New York: Workman Publishing Co., 1996). A book filled with practical help and valuable information for adult children caring for aging parents.

Humanity Comes of Age: The New Context for Ministry With the Elderly, by Susanne S. Paul and James A. Paul (Geneva, Switzerland: World Council of Churches, 1994). An excellent resource for gaining insight and knowledge about a global perspective of aging.

Mature Years (Nashville: Cokesbury). A large-print quarterly magazine for older adults that is filled with articles and a Bible study based on the International Lessons.

A Ministry of Caring, by Duane A. Ewers (Nashville: Discipleship Resources, 1999). A skill training course divided into eleven sessions for helping laity in a ministry of caring. There is both a leader's guide and a participant's workbook.

No Wrinkles on the Soul: A Book of Readings for Older Adults, by Richard L. Morgan (Upper Room Books, 1990). Each of these sixty-two devotions offers a Scripture passage, a short meditation, a reading for reflection, and a prayer.

The Power of the Dream: Looking Forward in the Later Years, by Marie White Webb (Nashville: Abingdon Press, 1999). A moving testimony of faithful living in the later years.

Remembering Your Story: Creating Your Own Spiritual Autobiography (Revised Edition), by Richard L. Morgan (Nashville: Upper Room Books, 2002). Designed for small groups, this revised resource encourages and guides participants through ten sessions of life review and future direction. There is a leader's guide and a participant's workbook.

Rock of Ages: A Worship and Songbook for Retirement Living (Nashville: Discipleship Resources, 2002). A large-print ecumenical songbook and worship guide for use in nursing homes, retirement communities, hospitals, homes, and other older-adult settings

Senior Adult Ministry in the 21st Century: Step-By-Step Strategies for Reaching People Over 50, by David P. Gallagher (Loveland, CO: Group Publishing, 2002). This helpful resource provides step-by-step strategies for reaching people over fifty years of age.

Soulful Aging: Ministry Through the Stages of Adulthood, by Henry C. Simmons and Jane Wilson (Macon: Smyth & Helwys, 2001). A ministry resource for older adults as they journey through the later years of life.

Successful Aging: The MacArthur Foundation Study, by John W. Rowe, M.D., and Robert L. Kahn, Ph.D (New York: Random House, Inc., 1998). A good book about lifestyle choices that, according to the authors, are more important than genes in determining how well we age.

A Very Present Help: Psalm Studies for Older Adults, by Miriam Dunson (Louisville: Geneva Press, 1999). A valuable resource for use with Bible study groups and individuals.

Winter Grace: Spirituality and Aging, by Kathleen Fischer (Nashville: Upper Room Books, 1998). A classic book showing how the losses that accompany aging can lead to freedom and new life.

With Faces to the Evening Sun: Faith Stories From the Nursing Home, by Richard L. Morgan (Nashville: Upper Room Books, 1998). A large-print book filled with meditations that are especially useful for nursing home residents, their families, and staff.